M000198801

CONGA & LU

THE CHRONICLES OF TWO CUBANAS

A SILENT KISS GOODBYE

CONGA & LU

THE CHRONICLES OF TWO CUBANAS

A SILENT KISS GOODBYE

Cuba Giblin
Monet Layton

gatekeeper press™

Columbus, Ohio

All of the events in this book are true and are written to the best of authors' recollections.

The views and opinions expressed in this book are solely those of the authors and do not reflect the views or opinions of Gatekeeper Press. Gatekeeper Press is not to be held responsible for and expressly disclaims responsibility of the content herein.

Conga & Lu: The Chronicles of Two Cubanas

Published by Gatekeeper Press
2167 Stringtown Rd, Suite 109
Columbus, OH 43123-2989
www.GatekeeperPress.com

Copyright © 2021 by Cuba Giblin, Monet Layton & Havana Layton
All rights reserved. Neither this book, nor any parts within it, may be sold or reproduced in any form or by any electronic or mechanical means, including information storage and retrieval systems, without permission in writing from the authors. The only exception is by a reviewer, who may quote short excerpts in a review.

The cover design for this book is entirely the product of the authors. Gatekeeper Press did not participate in and is not responsible for any aspect of this element.

Library of Congress Control Number: 2020944670

ISBN (hardcover): 9781662904080
ISBN (paperback): 9781662904097
eISBN: 9781662904103

For Mamy y Papy
For us

"Day and night I always dream with open eyes."
— José Martí

Contents

Chapter 1

Lu

Hidden behind the banister, I see her, and I want to get closer.
I can't hear what she's saying, and I need to know more.
I catch glimpses of her dimples as she speaks to my mother.
I notice her dark skin.
Her white dress.
She is perfect.

I sneak down the first two stairs, hoping to get a better view.
I am fast, but not careful.
I drop the bag, and my jacks crash down to the bottom of the
   winding staircase.
Some even make it all the way to the ground.
One by one they scatter across the floor.
The tiny pink ball reaches the bottom of the stairs, then bounces
   from one black square to the next.
I hurry to retrieve the game before being noticed.
Too late.

I hear a giggle, and I look up to see her kneeling next to me on the
   marble tile, scooping up the teeny jacks, some still spinning
   like petite ballerinas.
She looks at me and reveals a gorgeous smile.
It shines like a light.
Mamy shouts for me to go upstairs.

I know she can't see me, but she knows I was down there … spying.
The enchanting visitor hands me the last jack, winks, and whispers,
    "My name is Iluminada."

"Iluminada. Iluminada. Iluminada."
I repeat the name over and over in my head.
It sounds magical.
The light, "Iluminada."
I wish I could say it as rhythmically as she did.
It had rolled off her tongue so gracefully.
It is exquisite and intriguing.
It means enlightened.
Although I'm young, I already know.
This woman is special.

I reach the top of the stairs and tell my brother she is the one.
He is doubtful, but I know.
"Her name is Illuninanda. No, Ilulinana. No … her name is Lu,"
    I tell him.
I hear the thud of our front door closing, and I sprint back down
    the stairs.
I race towards the study.
"Hire her, Mamy."

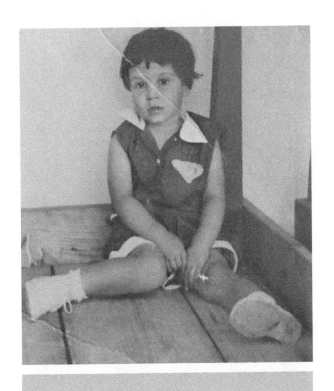

CUBA PÉREZ-SILVA

Chapter 2

The Interview

My steps are small as I walk down the short concrete entrance to the mansion in front of me. The house is massive. I knock two times on the large wooden door. A petite, striking woman opens the door. She is perfectly polished and exudes grace.

"*Hola*, my name is Iluminada."

"Yes, come in," she says.

There is an enormous oil painting of Jesus and a lengthy table with too many chairs to count. Exquisite furnishings are everywhere. The hallway is endless. I follow her to a library filled with hundreds of books. I sit, and although I am thirsty, I do not ask for a drink.

"Thank you for coming. You were highly recommended by the Almendres family. Your primary responsibility will be to care for our two children. As a domestic, your other duties will be to clean and tidy the house. This includes laundry and washing the dishes throughout the day. You are also expected to prepare lunches and dinners. There is an

4

apartment in the back of the house. It is very comfortable. You may live there. You will be paid $35 every month. Room and board is included along with your pay. Wednesday nights we will need you to stay longer. Saturdays and Sundays are your days off," she says. The *señora* excuses herself and says she will be back momentarily.

While I wait, I hear a clatter. To my right are a pair of tiny brown eyes, staring. She frantically collects jacks from the floor. I rush to help her. "My name is Iluminada."

She smiles, waves, then runs upstairs. I quickly return to my chair, ready to finish the interview. I can already tell I want this job.

ILUMINADA VIDAL

Chapter 3

CARDECUYOTU

Our house in Havana is grand.
My grandfather, Abuelo Delio, had it built for all of his children.
When his children had families of their own, he kept adding on to
    the house so his children could live with their families here.
Our entire family could be together.

Our house was built with love.
A love a man had for his wife.
A young couple who had moved to Havana to begin a journey with
    their new family.
My grandfather even named our house CARDECUYOTU, by
    taking the first part of each of his children's names.
CARmen, DElio, CUba (my Mamy), YOlanda, and TUlio.
This name proudly adorns its stucco facade.

I love living in CARDECUYOTU.
Calle Figueroa 362.
There is always something to do and someone to play with.
We run up and down the stairs.
We dart in and out of the seemingly endless number of bedrooms
    playing hide and seek.

Sometimes we see my father straightening his tie, getting ready
for work.
Sometimes we catch my uncle kissing his girlfriend on the bed.
Sometimes we hear Aunt Chucha weeping by her mirror.
Sometimes we uncover secrets.
Sometimes we tell our own.

I watch my grandmother create beautiful original paintings in her suite.
My favorites are the Oriental canvases of Asians with full bodies
in pastel colors.
They are a stark contrast to the religious scenes she captures with
dark, vibrant paint.
I sit in the back patio under the mighty mamey tree and watch the
ants crawl up its massive trunk.

We play hopscotch on the porch as my grandpa smokes cigars,
watching everything from his rocking chair.
The porch is constantly in motion — it is never still.
From dawn till dusk the rocking chairs made of Cuban mahogany
beckon all those who pass by on Figueroa Street to stop, sit,
rock, and chat with the Silvas.
The front doors are always open, and we are in the park until we
see the moon.
It is our signal that it's time to go home.

CARDECUYOTU is majestic.
Its white pillars welcome everyone —
Cuban Presidents, diplomats, teachers, and paupers.
But today it welcomes Lu.
My pleading and begging had worked.
My parents agreed to hire Iluminada.

She will be my *manejadora*, my nanny.

Today is her first day.

I see her from my upstairs window, clutching her small black bag.

I hurry down to greet her, but instead of entering the house she walks down the thin brick driveway towards the back of our home to the tiny apartment above the garage.

This is where she will keep her things and stay at night.

I wish she could be in one of the many bedrooms of the main house, but it's OK.

I am happy that she is here.

I cannot wait to learn more about her.

CARDECUYOTU

ABUELA CUBA, YOLANDA, ABUELO DELIO - CHUCHO, TULIO, CHUCHA, CUBITA

Chapter 4

Matanzas

I was born January 16, 1932, in the province of Matanzas. It is a land of hills, rivers, bridges, beaches, and baseball. I grew up in a small farm town, Sabanilla de Comendador, in a humble home with my parents and many brothers and sisters. Our land has an abundance of fruit trees. Every morning my mother prepared fresh fruit. I loved climbing the trees. My mother says I have a knack for finding perfect mangoes. I would shimmy up the large trees with ease and touch each fruit to see how soft they were. Then I would smell them. The smell tells you if they are ready to be plucked. I made sure never to toss them down. I made baskets from my handkerchiefs and gently carried them down. This protected them so they would never have soft spots or bruises.

Childhood was hard but happy. I remember we visited Cuevas de Bellamar. The rock formations deep underground looked otherworldly. Some rocks looked like melting icicles. The caves had lakes like clear crystal, and we took turns jumping in. Sometimes we went to the beach, down the steep streets and past the sugar mills to the valley. When we were lucky, tiny crabs mating by the shore waved their claws, marching like they were in a parade. It was an unforgettable sight. Thousands of red crabs taking over. It always made us laugh. The magnificent beaches in Matanzas are the most beautiful in the world.

I miss my home and family, but there is limited opportunity in Sabanilla de Comendador. Some of my friends have gone to Havana in search of work, as I have. They found jobs in nightclubs and hotels. It was a difficult decision. At fifteen, I said goodbye to my mother, father, brothers, and sisters, and to each of the three rivers of my birthplace. I took the bus into Havana filled with optimism for the opportunities that awaited me.

I was first employed by a family living in the elegant Miramar neighborhood. For two years, I took care of three children and worked in the house, but I was never really happy, disconnected from the family. Later, I worked for another family in La Sierra as a caretaker and a domestic. I cooked, cleaned, and cared for the baby they just brought home. It was a good job. I grew attached to the baby, Maria. But after five years the family moved to Argentina. Great possibilities came when I heard a prominent family was looking to hire help with their household in La Víbora.

I am certain God has chosen the right path for me. He has led me to this house in Havana, CARDECUYOTU. I will work here to support my family in Matanzas.

So far everyone here is very nice. This house is enormous. It belongs to the Silvas. Señor Delio and his wife Cuba live downstairs. They added on whole houses and built a second story for their family. I am working upstairs for one of their daughters, Señora Cubita. She is very elegant. She is businesslike and a bit terse, but I see she has a love for her family that is real and true. She married Señor René. He is very intelligent and talkative. Sometimes he tells me to sit, and we chat about all subjects. I am fond of the children that I care for. There is Neny, a boy who is six years old, and his little sister Cuby is barely five. It has only been a short time, but I have already bonded with Cuby. I call her Conga, and she calls me Lu. She brings me joy.

Chapter 5

Conga

Lu is unlike any of the other *manejadoras* I have had.
She is in her twenties.
Her face is round and kind.
Her chocolate skin is smooth, and her eyes shine like black
sapphires.
Her short hair is always up in a handkerchief.
She's vibrant, fun, and happy.

In the morning I can't wait to get up.
I jump out of my bed and follow the music, because I know it will
lead me to her.
She is sweeping the checkered floor and dancing with her broom.
The radio is loud and playing *Vacilón, qué rico vacilón, cha cha
cha, qué rico cha cha cha.*
Her movements are mesmerizing.
She passes me the broom, and I dance, too.
I sway my hips back and forth to the beat.
I try to imitate her dancing.
She shows me how to dance the Conga, one of Cuba's most famous
dances.
We march rhythmically together.
I drag my feet and move my hips and shoulders as best as I can to
the rhythm.

Conga & Lu

"Conga," she says. "Yes, I'll call you Conga."
We sway, sing, and laugh while she works.

When she finishes the dusting, she brings out a jigsaw puzzle.
I find my own space nestled in close to her.
We take turns adding pieces.
My brother comes in dressed like a cowboy chasing after my
    cousin Tulito.
They ride their "horses" right through the middle of the puzzle.
It breaks apart into dozens of pieces. All our work is destroyed.
It looks just as it did when it first came out of the box.
Tears form in my eyes, and the salty drops fall onto the floor.

Lu is there to pick up the pieces.
She tells me to put my cowgirl outfit on.
I struggle to pull the red boots over my ankles.
Lu helps, and I am ready.

Las Vaqueras — the cowgirls.
We saddle up on our brooms and ride off into the sunset.
I look behind to see my brother and Tulito frowning.
They are forced to clean up the puzzle.

Yee-haw.

CUBY   RENY   CUBY

YOLY, RENY, CUBY, CARMEN, RENECITO

COUSINS

17

Chapter 6

The Silvas

The Silvas are not like other families.

The names of the family are steeped in tradition and history.

Delio Silva, my grandfather, was born in Morón, Camagüey in 1896.

He had two brothers, Anibal and Aristides, and one sister, Elida.

He married my grandmother, Cuba Herrera Herrera.

My Abuela Cuba had two sisters and three brothers — Rafael, José Maria, and Juan.

Her family left Cuba to seek refuge in Tampa during the Spanish-American War.

Her parents had twins while exiled in Tampa in the United States.

They named one daughter Cuba and their other daughter Florida as a way to honor both their homeland and the state that welcomed them to safety.

They had their third daughter when they returned to Cuba.

They named her America.

Cuba is my grandmother, my *abuela*.

I love to hear her talk about the olden days.

She was born in 1897, an entire century before me.

They had no electricity, no cars, no televisions, no telephones!

Abuela is a strong woman.

She is the pillar of our family, the glue that holds us together.

She is tough, smart, proper, and serious.

When she talks we listen.

Growing up in El Vedado in Havana, she was the daughter of a wealthy businessman.

She wanted to be a physician.

Her father told her that women were not meant to be doctors.

He didn't allow her to pursue that career, but her brother José Maria did become a physician.

Abuela thought a pharmacist was the next best thing.

She went to college and became a Doctor of Pharmacy.

In the early 1900s, this was almost unheard of for a woman.

After earning her degree, she chose to be the pharmacist at the jail in Havana.

She proves women are capable of anything.

She is fearless.

Abuela is short and pale.

She never sits in the sun.

She is an excellent cook, a talented painter, a good judge of character, and most importantly she will do anything for her family.

She is a true renaissance woman.

She is also my hero.

She married my grandfather, Delio, President of the *Tribunal Supremo Popular de Cuba*, the Supreme Court.

They have five children: Carmen, Delio, Cuba (my mother), Yolanda, and Tulio.

My mamy and papy met at the courthouse building in downtown Havana.

We call it *El Bureau*.

Mamy didn't need to work.

The Silvas are very wealthy and well off.

But Mamy wanted an occupation.

She is always on the go.

Her father worked at the tribunal, so she became a judicial secretary.

Every day at 4:55 p.m. she would enter the elevator, and the Chinese bell hop would greet her.

He would check his watch and announce "*Chinco meno chinco*" — five minutes till 5:00 — as if he were telling her she was leaving too early.

My mother was amused by the way he said "chinco" instead of *cinco*, so she figured she'd get to hear it twice if she left at 4:55.

One day on one of these elevator rides down to the lobby, she met the handsome and charismatic judge, Dr. René Pérez-Amargos.

He asked her name, to which she replied, "Cuba."

"Uva," he said, "What a beautiful name."

Uvas are grapes.

Mamy felt he'd be embarrassed if she corrected him, so she let him call her *Uva* for days.

When Papy came to CARDECUYOTU for the first time, he was not up to the Silva standard.

Abuela looked at him and told my mother, "He has poor constitution."

Mamy didn't care.

She loved René.

He also soon won over each one of the Silvas.

Cubita and René married and have two children: My brother René (Neny or Renito), and Cuba (me, Cuby).

Our family always names the firstborn girl after their mother, and the firstborn boy after their father.

In the Silva family, we have three Cubas: Cuba, my abuela; Cubita, my mamy; and Cuby, me.

Three Delios: Delio, my abuelo; Chucho; and Chuchin.

Four Renés: René, René, Renecito, and Renito.

Two Carmens: Chucha and Carmenchu.

Two Tulios: Tulio and Tulito.

Two Rogelios: Cuco and Cuquito.

Two Yolandas: Yolanda and Yoly.

Two Hortensias: Hortensia and Tensy.

And one Isabel: Nena, Tulito's mother.

When Chuchin and Tensy's mother Hortensia died, Chuchin lived in CARDECUYOTU with Abuela.

Tensy went to live with Hortensia's sister Olga and her husband Tony.

Their son is also named Tony, but we call him Tonito — another cousin!

Their house is near ours.

They are with us on most of our vacations, and we see them nearly every day.

Luckily, we all have nicknames.

CHUCHO, TULIO, ABUELO DELIO, CUCO, RENÉ (PAPY), RENÉ
HORTENSIA
NENA, ABUELA CUBA, CHUCHA, CUBITA (MAMY), YOLANDA
TULITO, CUBY (ME), RENY (NENY)
RENECITO, CHUCHIN, TENSY, CARMENCHU, YOLY

MAMY

PAPY

Chapter 7

Manejadoras

All of us have *manejadoras*, our nannies.

I had a few before Lu.

I don't remember her name, but I knew the last one smelled like
wilted flowers, body odor, and onions.

She was cold, portly, and sleepy.

She was always cross.

The wrinkles of her forehead formed an "X" between her eyes.

Her skin was pale and white, and she had messy brown hair that
looked like the inside of a coconut.

My father would complain about her onion soup, "*Hay pero sopa
de cebolla otra vez!*"

Yes, it was onion soup again.

She must have thought it was very tasty …

All I remember is that it made me gag with every sip, and
I "accidentally" spilled it often.

My cousins all have *manejadoras,* too.

Fela is my cousin Carmenchu's and Cuquito's nanny.

She is young and pretty like Lu.

Dominica is Tensy and Chuchin's.

She is very big and round.

She is fine, but boring.

She never plays with us.

Renecito and Yoly's house seems to have a revolving door when it
    comes to nannies.
They are always having someone new look after them.
I think they are on their fourth one already.
Lu told me she heard that they all quit because Renecito is a terror.
When Renecito arrives the park, all the other *manejadoras* quickly
    gather up their children and leave, saying, "Here he comes!"
I wonder how long Caridad, his current nanny, will stay?

Dulce is my cousin Tulito's *manejadora*.
Her name means *sweet* in English, but she is as sour as they come.
We call her the Wicked Witch of the West.
If anything is broken, she always blames me.
I feel like she hates us as much as we hate her.
But she treats Tulito like a prince.
Even though he is the one that gets into the most trouble, we are
    the ones that she scolds.
She is bossy, boring, and unpleasant, to say the least.
The rumor is that her son killed someone, but she took the blame.
She went to jail.
My grandmother, Abuela, felt sorry for her and used her
    connections to set her free.
Then she hired her as a nanny for Tulito, her grandson.
Dulce gives me the creeps, and I try to stay away from her.

I see them sitting and watching.
They all wear the same white dresses.
They sit on concrete park benches chatting while we take turns
    gliding down the silver slide.
Lu says she likes to wear her mandatory uniform, so she doesn't
    have to soil her real clothes.

They chat and laugh with each other, yet are still very attentive to
us children.
I wave to Lu, and she waves back.
Thank God Lu is mine.

Lu doesn't even like onions.

PEPE
BELEN
FELA ↑
FRIJOLITO (FRANCISCO)
& DULCE
AT TARARA

FELA, CUQUITO, CARMENCHU, TENSY, TULITO, CHUCHIN, RENECITO, & EL PILLO
CARIDAD AND YOLY

Chapter 8

She Doesn't See My Skin

Cuba has negros, whites, mulatos, morenos, and mestizos. For the most part, blacks live together in certain neighborhoods and whites live in their neighborhoods. The beaches and dance clubs I go to are open to negros. My favorite beaches are *Santa Fe* and *Guanabano*. Whites have their own night clubs, yacht clubs, and beaches. They go to the Miramar Yacht Club, the Biltmore, or the Havana Yacht Club, to name a few. To be honest, I have no interest in them; they seem dull, pretentious, and fake. Our black clubs are the exciting ones, filled with laughter, life, jazz, dancing, and energy. I find comfort in the familiar. We are the black beans, and they are the white rice.

Moros is a dish named after how the African Moors (the black beans) mixed with the *Cristianos* from Spain (the white rice). When I prepare the dish, I make sure to always add extra beans, because it is the beans that give it flavor. Everything is better with a little more color.

Solares are mostly inhabited by blacks. I find the realness of life in the shanties — the bright colors of laundry drying in the wind, singing, music, the smell of fried garlic and onions escaping through cracks in the windows. With my friends who live in the *solares,* I don't have to say, "*Si, señora*." I say, "*Qué pasa*?" We share a connection and culture that I miss. Blacks are mostly ignored by the whites in Cuba. It's as if we are invisible to them.

While I live at CARDECUYOTU, Señora Cubita, Señor René, and all the adults in the house see me. They also see my blackness. But not Conga. She doesn't see my skin. She sees my smile, she sees my laugh, she sees my love. She holds my hand. She sits in my lap. She hugs me tightly. Conga lives her life in color, yet she does not see color. She is a very special girl.

Most affluent neighborhoods in Havana don't have many black residents. I wonder why there are not more negros in high-paying jobs with important titles. I feel the black community needs to put more emphasis on education. Schooling is very important. Señor René told me once, "With education comes opportunity." I am content in my life, but when I am a mother, I will teach the value of education to my children. If they want more in this life, education will be their way to advance.

There are invisible lines that divide Cubans. Cubans are separated by race, but there is also a stark divide between the wealthy and the poor. The rich in Cuba socialize with the rich. Those who are cane cutters or service workers are found together. We are separated by our social class. It's just the way it is.

Chapter 9

La Bonita

I walk with Lu to *La Bonita*, the corner store.
We go before the Cuban sun heats up the streets.
Before the flowers are fully open.
Before the birds finish their morning songs.

We are on the hunt for things Mamy needs.
Some days Mamy hands Lu a list of what she needs.
Some days Mamy phones in her order.
Many of our neighbors do not have a telephone — we are lucky to
    have one.
The wall between my house and Carmenchu's has a small cutout.
It is a small opening that the phone sits in, so, both of our families
    can use it.
Cuquito and I are the smallest, so we often crawl through the hole
    to get to each other's houses.
It is especially helpful when our parents forget their keys inside.
We love pretending we are secret agents sent on special missions.

I love La Bonita, but I don't like it when Mamy sends us to *El
    Carnicero.*
It is on the other corner.
The meat market smells like blood.
Everything is way too fresh.

Lu chooses the chicken she wants, and the butcher quickly snaps
    its neck.
Then we carry it home to cook.
Neither of us ever likes going there.
But luckily today it is *La Bonita*.

Our walk is not just a walk; it is an adventure.
I take several steps down the sidewalk for every one of hers.
We pass another *manejadora* pushing a white stroller with a crying
    baby.
We sing and skip hand-in-hand until we get to the store.
Lu takes the neatly written list out of her pocket.
She tells me to find the *mantequilla*.
I love butter.
It's creamy, smooth, and salty.
I like to watch the designs it makes when I butter my bread and dip
    it into my *café con leche*.
The oil swirls, and I paint in my tiny coffee cup.
Abuelo says it helps lubricate our joints and keeps our bodies
    running smoothly.
I never see him exercise, but I always see him with his *cafecito*.
Sometimes I scoop up butter with my spoon and I eat it like ice cream.
Qué rico!

Bananas, plantains, mangos, milk, AHHH BUTTER.
I grab it and quickly bring it to Lu.
She crosses it off the list.
We collect the other items that Mamy needs and go to the counter.
"*Hasta mañana*," says the clerk.
He knows we will be back tomorrow.

On the way home we look for squirrels, lizards, birds, and other
  creatures.
We find a woodpecker.
We name him Lido.
I get almost close enough to touch him, but with a flutter of his
  wings he is gone.
I follow him, my arms outstretched, and I flap my wings.

"It's time to go Conga," Lu says. "The butter is melting."

CAFECITO

Chapter 10

My Day

Fela and I wake up to the sounds of Benny Moré. She enjoys music as much as I do. Fela and I are great roommates. We share the apartment over the garage at CARDECUYOTU. We shower, put on our crisp white linen uniforms, and go to our respective homes to start our day. Working for Señor René and Señora Cubita is pleasant. My typical day consists of cooking, cleaning, and taking care of the children. I manage the household. I enter the kitchen at 8:00 and inhale the aroma of the *cafecitos* and fresh-baked Cuban bread. The family is already sitting at the dining room table having their breakfast. Neny and Conga are having "bread fights," throwing the inside white *masa* of the bread at each other. After greeting them and a hug from Conga, I sit at the kitchen table and delight in my morning *café con leche*.

My day begins and ends with music. The kitchen's back door is open, and I listen to the melodic chirps of the wild birds. I sweep and wash the tile floors as the radio plays some Cuban cha-cha-cha. The bathroom is next. Conga and Neny's room is a bit of a mess

34

this morning. They must have had Carmenchu and Cuquito over last night. After making the beds and straightening the toys on the shelf, I move to the master bedroom. Señora Cubita has many oriental ceramic pieces. They are fragile and delicate. I have to be very careful as I dust the fisherman with the fish hanging on its thin pole. Señora Cubita also collects unique Lladró figurines. They adorn the shelves on the living room walls. *La sala* (the living room), dining room, hallway, and back room come next. The home has the latest modern amenities. It is one of the only houses in the neighborhood with an electric washing machine. I don't know any other houses on the block with the modern amenities we have!

I finish hanging the laundry outside to dry on the clothesline in the patio. Finally, the house chores are completed. But I must not forget the bunnies! Conga has many rabbits that live in her father's study. They are city bunnies — very well trained to soil only in their box. I give them a once over and greet them by name. Mama bunny looks to be making a space for her soon-to-be-born litter of babies. Conga is going to be thrilled.

"*Mi amor*, it's time to take a walk to La Bonita," I say. Conga runs and puts her red Keds on. I swear if that child had her way, she would live shirtless and shoeless. She always wins the argument when she explains how unfair it is that boys can go shirtless and girls can't.

Today we walk on the opposite sidewalk. We never know what we will find. When we are done with our daily purchases, Conguita looks through the candy jars and picks a colorful treat.

We get home and begin *el almuerzo*, our midday meal. Conga helps me wash the lettuce. She is so small that she has to stand on a kitchen stool to reach the sink. She soon tires of her "job" and goes to play *cuquitas* (paper dolls) with her cousin Carmenchu. Today I am serving red beans and rice, *bistec empanizado* (breaded steak), and *malanga* (a tuber). For dessert I make *merenguitos* — *a sweet* favorite of the family. Everyone comes home for lunch. Then it's back to school for Neny, and Señor René goes back to work.

My afternoon is slow and easy. As I walk down the hall, I hear the phone ringing. "*Oigo*," I answer. We share a phone with Señora Chucha and her family. I write down a message for Señor René.

The house comes alive after 5:00 when everyone is home. Everyone really enjoys their time together. I listen to each of their stories and laugh as I prepare the evening meal. Señor René always has everyone on the edge of their seats, as he involves them in discussions and stories.

Señora Cuba always says the best appliances are Frigidaire. Upgrading the kitchen is an art for her. Today I am making Conga's favorite, *picadillo con mariquitas*, and bean puree for the children. The children like it better when their beans are mashed.

After I serve the evening meal and clean up the kitchen, my day is done! I hurry to meet my friends and coworkers Fela, Hilda, and Belen. We sit at the corner park bench. We talk, laugh, and gossip about the day. We chat about our weekend plans. Saturdays and Sundays are our days off. Dancing usually calls out to me on Saturday nights. On Sunday afternoons I take a bus to the beach and swim in the cool refreshing waters. My family in Matanzas is never forgotten. Next week I will spend the weekend at home. I will go shopping Saturday for them. My mother loves chocolates. I always bring her a box of sweets. My father loves cigars. My friend Juan in la Habana Vieja has access to the finest and hand picks a nice one for me to bring to him. My father's weakness is a tight-rolled cigar. My family loves the city gifts I bring home. Life is easy. Life is good.

Conga & Lu

SEÑORA CUBITA'S FIGURINES

RENY & CUBY

Chapter 11

The Baptism

It's Sunday.
No music in the morning
But I get to be with Papy and Mamy all day.
I sit with my parents and kick my brother under the table.
I dip my pan into my *cafecito.*
The bread soaks up the sweet, bold coffee, and I know I must get
    ready for mass soon.
But I resist for as long as I can.

We walk to our church, a chapel in *Los Maristas* school.
If we don't go every Sunday, then it is almost certain we will end
    up in hell.
Only the women and children attend the mass.
All the ladies sit and kneel, their heads covered in white lace veils.
I sit next to Mamy on the pew.
I see her fingers rolling over her rosary.
My mind wanders.
I don't understand any of the mass, since it is in Latin.
It seems like we are there a long time.
Even though the benches are wooden, I am comfortable.
I smell Mamy's perfume, a mix of flowers and honey.
Her bottle says Chanel #5.
I hear some familiar words, but I don't know what they mean.

Conga & Lu

No singing, just chanting.
Then I drift asleep as I count the pieces of stained glass in the
    window.

I wake up to a kiss on my head.
Mamy takes my hand, and we head outside.
We walk back home but stay in our nice clothes.

"Time for the baptism," my cousin Carmenchu says.
On Sundays we perform our own ceremonies for the new dolls.
The boys run away.
They do not want to play with dolls.
But we need them to be the priests and the husbands.
I decorate the patio with big palm leaves, while Carmenchu sets
    the table under the giant mamey tree.
Today it is Yoly's doll, Maria, who will be baptized.

"We have treats!" we say in unison to lure the boys to the back.
Tonito is the first to agree.
Soon after the others come running.
Although they are sweaty and underdressed for the sacrament,
    they will do.
The large sink in the back is perfect.
We dunk Maria into the white porcelain bowl.
My cousin Renecito says a prayer.

We sit and eat the meal consisting of mango, candies, and
    chocolates from La Bonita.
Soon it is nearly 3:00 and time for our Sunday dinner.
Today paella is on the menu, but I know Abuela will have something
    else made for us kids.

The entire family, about thirty of us, meet in my grandmother's formal dining room downstairs.

Abuela rings the bell to let her chef, Frijolito, know that we are ready to eat.

We call him "Frijolito," because the hair on his head resembles little black beans.

We always try to see what's going on in the kitchen, but he doesn't like us bothering him.

He chases us out, and we run around outside.

The kitchen has swinging doors just like the fancy restaurants do.

We love to run in one door and come out the other.

The table is expansive.

There are twenty-two chairs.

I sit with all the other kids at the table next to the big one.

I often wonder when it will be my time to sit with the adults.

My brother and cousin Chuchin tell jokes about Pepito as I make tiny sandwiches by scooping beans, rice, and picadillo onto the crispy plantains.

Frijolito makes good plantain chips, but Lu's are better.

We hear our parents laughing, swearing, joking, and telling stories next to us.

Our bellies are full, and we are happy.

POMPEYO, IRAIDA, CUBA, MAMY, RENY, PAPY, DELIO

YOLY, CUBY, TENSY, CARMEN

Chapter 12

Mother's Day

I enjoy preschool.
"Let's go," I say as I tug on Lu's dress. "*Vamos.*"
After she feeds me breakfast, we head out.
My tiny feet move so much faster than hers.

Americusa's preschool is on Avenida Santa Catalina.
It is in an enormous house.
The school is downstairs, and Americusa herself lives upstairs.
As soon as we get there, I run to the garage to get my chair.
There are about a dozen stacked small wooden chairs.
I take some down and carefully check their front sides.
They each have a painting of an animal on them, but only one has
    the horsey.
I get there just in time.
Everyone wants the horsey, so you have to be quick.
Today the horsey is mine.
I ride my chair from the garage and into the classroom.
"*Adios*, Lu," I say.

Almost everyone in the neighborhood comes to Americusa's.
My cousin Renecito had started there.
He told us he hated it.
My Aunt Yolanda would have to drag him kicking and screaming
    all the way.

He grabbed onto bushes, cars, anything.
Yolanda would have to pry his hands free and pull him along.
He eventually behaved so badly that he was thrown out.

My brother was also an exception.
My father brought him to Americusa's when he was four.
After a few minutes Papy pulled him out and told Americusa that
he was too advanced to be cutting paper flowers.
Off he went to *Los Maristas* for kindergarten, with the priests in
the long black cloaks.

We are getting ready for our Mother's Day Pageant.
I am usually the first Dame.
I don't like it, but at least I'm not the Queen.
I hate the pageants, but Mamy loves them.
I am forced to wear huge frilly dresses.
Parents clap, and the newspaper comes to take photographs.
All the children do a little show.

Mother's Day is always a big spectacle.
Weeks before Mother's Day, Mamy and I would go downtown to
pick out fabric that we would bring to our seamstress.
She would design and sew our matching dresses for the occasion.
All the moms and daughters wore matching dresses.
We would go to mass at *Los Maristas*.
If your mom was alive, you wore a bright red rose on your lapel
or dress.
If your mom had died, you would wear a beautiful white rose.
I always felt sad for everyone who had to have a white rose pinned
to them, especially for my cousins Tensy and Chuchin, whose
mother Hortensia died when they were young.

I sit quietly and cut paper flowers that will be used as decorations
for the stage.
Before long Lu picks me up.
I can smell the scent of garlic and oil on her clothes.
When I get home, it will be time for lunch.

I can already taste the plantain chips.

Dia de las Madres

11 de Mayo de 1958
COLEGIO CHAMPAGNAT
Víbora - Habana

CHUCHA & CARMENCHU MATCHING DRESSES

MOTHER'S DAY PAGEANT

CUBY – MOTHER'S DAY

CUADRO DE HONOR
DEL
KINDERGARTEN No. 157
CURSO ESCOLAR DE

RENY, CUBY, MAMY

Chapter 13

My Weekends

Saturday and Sunday are my days off. It's Saturday, so I take the bus into downtown Havana. Dancing calls to me on Saturday nights. I have several favorite spots. Last weekend I danced at *Club Polar* and *El Estadio de la Tropical*. Today I decide on *Union Fraternas*. As I arrive, Mario is in his usual spot outside, smoking on the curb. I open the door, and a wave of music engulfs me. Dancing is my release. I wear what I want to wear and say what I want to say. I am free.

I order a beer. I never go for the hard stuff. I take a few sips and begin dancing. It is hot. I love feeling the sweat trickle down the back of my neck and the heat from the bodies moving around me. It energizes me, and my heart beats rapidly. The music is loud as the trumpet squeals. I make my way to the bar for a few more sips of my beer. I am happy.

The tall handsome man on the stool beside me asks me to dance. I smile and nod. He takes my hand and pulls me back to the dance floor. Our hips move rhythmically to the beat of the

drums. We dance the *danzón*. Is it the cerveza?
Is it the music? Is it the man? I don't know,
but I feel alive. I want to cha-cha until the
morning. I hope the night never ends.

ILUMINADA

Chapter 14

El Comodoro

It is summertime in Havana.

Yolanda is always the driver. The men are at work.

We load up the car and head to *El Comodoro*, our yacht club.

Most people that we know belong to the club. It isn't far, just a short drive from our house.

All my cousins are members, except for Carmenchu and Cuquito.

They belong to the Miramar Yacht Club.

It is next to *El Comodoro*.

They say it is fancier, but I know Carmenchu likes ours better, since we are all there.

As soon as we arrive the game begins.

We try to run past the front receptionist without being seen.

Ughh the *comemierda* is there again.

He thinks he's guarding the presidential palace.

We never want to stop to show our membership cards.

Whoever is caught must pay our penalty or complete a dare of our choosing.

Yoly loses.

She is spotted by the short man in the front.

We laugh because she will have to do the dare.

We rush towards the pool.

We decide that for her dare Yoly must jump off the high dive.

We are all strong swimmers, but the high dive looks menacing.

Yoly is a bigger girl.
Our parents are always trying to make us eat.
They want us plump and puffy.
I am scrawny and skinny, but Yoly's body is soft and round.
She is always laughing and is the funniest one of the group.

"*No problema!*" she cheerfully states.
She steps up the ladder, her steps less confident as she approaches
    the top.
She tightens the straps of her swimsuit around her neck.
We are all waiting ... watching ....
We countdown 3, 2, 1 ....

She runs to the end of the board.
She is flying ....
She is falling ....
BUT she is not over the pool.
The entire club watches.
They peek out of their cabanas and gasp.

She hits the deck with a thud.
Her body bounces.
Then she is still.
Tonito is the first to reach her.
We expect the worst.
The concrete is broken and cracked.
The entire club is shocked ... silent ... solemn.
We wait.

As if she was a jack in the box, Yoly suddenly pops right up.
She opens her eyes and stares straight at us.

"What are you all waiting for? Race you to the beach," she says, as
     if nothing happened.
We are overjoyed but confused.
I think the extra cushion must've protected her.
I will eat my entire dinner tonight.
Maybe I'll even ask for seconds.

We run to the beach and rush into the water.
Only the American tourists lie on chairs and towels on the sand
     to try to get brown.
We laugh because most of them are red and peeling like the gumbo
     limbo trees.
I wonder why they find that look appealing?
The water feels so good.
Perfect actually.
I swim to the floating wooden *balsa.*
This raft-like deck is where we sit and play for hours.
We try to catch the colorful fish that swim between our legs.
It is like our own aquarium.
We are protected by the shark net.
We jump on and off.
No one is daring enough to cross over it.
Once a shark broke through the net, and it swam circles around
     the people on the balsa.
Luckily, we were not on the raft then.
We were on the shore.

Mamy always made us wait for two hours to go into the water after
     we ate.
She said if we didn't wait, we would get *embolia.*
I don't even know what *embolia* is, but I don't want it.

Next we sit on the concrete wall and dangle our toes into the water.
The wall divides the kids from the adults.
We sit and wait for a wave to crash over and carry us into the
    lagoon.
I see Mamy waving us in from the beach.
I hope the wave comes soon.
I look back and see one is forming perfectly.
We put our arms over our heads.
The crest is here. It lifts us and pushes us with a gentle force.
We are dolphins.
We ride the wave all the way to the sandy shore.

Our parents wrap us up in striped towels and give us our Cinzano
    Vermouth to warm up.
I wonder why we need to warm up.
It is Cuba and it is summer, but our parents still worry we will
    catch a cold.

Some days the boys do judo, but today we see they are going to have
    a swim competition.
None of us are part of the team, but anyone who is a member of
    the club can race.
We always enter the meets.
None of us were ever taught to swim.
We just have a knack, I guess.
The swim coach sees the seven of us coming.

"*Coño*," he mutters under his breath.
We always beat his swimmers.
Neny and I have never had a swim lesson.
We were just thrown into the ocean when we were very young.

The swimmers line up on the cement piers.
The boys race first.
Neny easily wins.
The coach shakes his head in humiliation.
Chuchin is second.
Tulito doesn't participate.
He watches and cheers.
Tulito hates swimming.
We dominate.

Girls are next.
I wait for the whistle.
I swim the whole way without taking a breath.
My heart beats fast as my arms churn through the water.
My feet propel me like engines.
I am the smallest and the youngest.
But I swim circles around my competition.
I finish in first place, too.
We stand on wooden boxes and the coach puts the medals around
    our necks.
He is so angry I think he may try to strangle me with it.
Mamy is so proud she cries.
The Silvas rule the pool.
I'm not even tired, so I challenge Neny to one more race.
I beat him, too.
I am fast and feisty.
The undisputed champion.

It's time for a cousin adventure.
We go to the docks where they keep the rowboats.

We decide we will row to the Miramar Yacht Club to see Carmenchu
and Cuquito.

It is not our luck.

The strict attendant is on duty.

He tells us that to take the boat today we need an adult.

The boys go ask our parent's friend Luisita.

She is a bit slow, and the boys know she will agree to come.

We row to Miramar.

It doesn't take long.

We find Carmenchu and Cuquito swimming before we even get
to the pier.

We tell them about Yoly and the diving board and about our
swimming victories.

We dive for sea urchins and bring them to the surface then watch
them sink back down to the bottom of the sea.

We laugh and splash but notice a raincloud forming over the ocean.

It is time to head back, but the boys purposely set sail without
Luisita.

She is running and waving on the dock.

We laugh and watch her flailing arms and hear her shouting for us
to stop and come back for her.

We know we will get in BIG trouble, but it is worth it.

We are free and on the high seas.

We don't have to rinse the salt and sand off of us.

We dance and sing "*Que llueva, que llueva, la Virgen de la Cueva.*"

Then we wait for our Cuban showers.

Around 3:00 the sky opens, and water pours from the clouds.

Conga & Lu

The rain is strong enough to wash away the beach from our bodies.
Neny finds a corner where the gutter ends.
The water builds up and makes a forceful spout.
Our own waterfall.

A few minutes later, the sun is out.
I love to watch the sun's heat evaporate the thin puddles left by the
    quick rain shower.
The steam comes off the roads and everything is clean.
I stare at the gold medal still hanging around my neck as we drive
    home in the car.
Tomorrow I may decide to go over the net.

The sharks can't catch me.

YOLANDA

HOTEL
Comodoro

Chapter 15

El Enano

Papy always drives home from the courthouse to eat lunch with us.
I love the stories he tells about the cases that he judges in his
courtroom.
I sit at the table while Lu prepares our meal.

"*Oigan escúchenme,*" he says. "Listen."
We are enchanted by his stories.
We listen intently.

He tells us about King Solomon from the Bible.
He recounts that there were two mothers living in the same
house.
Each was the mother of an infant boy.
The mothers went to Solomon after one of the infants was killed.
They both claimed that the baby who was still living was theirs.
Solomon asked for a sword.
He gave his judgement and said, "Since you both want this baby,
we will cut him in half. One of you can have the top half and
the other the bottom half."
The first woman did not protest the ruling and nodded in
agreement.
The second spoke up quickly and said, "Please give the boy to her,
just don't kill him!"

The king discerned right away the second woman was the true
   mother.
He knew a mother would do anything to save her child's life, even
   if it meant giving up her own baby.
He ruled the infant belonged to the second mother.

"Well *hijos*, today I have been bested," Papy said.
"I wish I could have been as wise as Solomon, but I have made an
   erroneous ruling."
I sit and wait. This is bound to be a fantastic story.

"*Un enano*, a dwarf, and a merchant came into my courtroom today.
   The shopkeeper accused the dwarf of stealing a gallon of milk
   and demanded he be paid in full for the milk he claimed was
   stolen. The dwarf, who was the defendant, proceeded to the
   bench. His lawyer, with my permission, placed a bottle of milk
   on my bench in the front of the courtroom. As the tiny man
   approached the bench it was revealed to me that he was not
   even as tall as you, Neny. He also had unusually short arms.
   All of his limbs were quite diminutive.

"'Your honor,' the dwarf began, 'how could someone of my size
   and stature possibly reach a bottle that high, then carry it
   off with my stubby little arms?' He began to try to reach and
   grab the milk off the table. He tried getting on his tippy toes,
   raising his arms up. He seemed to put every effort possible
   into obtaining the milk. He convinces me that he cannot grab
   it. After a few minutes of watching this scene, I announce
   my ruling. Pounding the bench with my gavel, I proclaim,
   '*Inocente*.'"

"'Thank you, your honor,' the dwarf said, as a massive grin spread across his face. He looked straight at me, then easily managed to grab the bottle of milk, tucked it haughtily under his arm, and walked straight out of the building. I was furious," Papy said.

My father is very wise.
He is astonished, and a bit embarrassed, that he was outsmarted in his courtroom.

"Lu, I think I'll have some milk," Neny says, as he grins slyly at Papy.

ABUELO SUPREME COURT OF CUBA

PAPY IN COURT

COMIENZAN A ESCRUTAR LAS JUNTAS MUNICIPALES ELECTORALES

PRESIDENTS GRAU & BATISTA & ABUELO

Chapter 16

Cumpleaños

Mamy says I must wear a dress.
I refuse.
I live in shorts.
My gangly legs show bruises and scrapes from roller-skating and
    climbing trees.
But birthdays are always celebrated the same way in our family.
Girls must wear dresses.
Boys dress in linen shirts and nice shoes.

One of the best things about birthday parties is the food.
The Jell-O with fruit, the *bocaditos* (tiny sandwiches), and my
    favorite — the *croquetas*.
My abuela's chicken *croquetas* are a tiny taste of heaven.
She fills each bite-sized, pill-shaped delicacy with just the right
    amount of *masa* then covers it with the finest powdered flour.
Each of Abuela's *croquetas* is exactly the same size.
They are my favorite, dainty and delicious.

Today it is my special day.
It's my birthday.
My brother and I go downstairs together and peek into the kitchen.
There it is!
It's spectacular.
My cake is a masterpiece.

The exquisite colors beckon us to come closer.

The bright pink, orange, and yellow frosting make it look like the Cuban sky during sunset.

No one will notice if we just sample a teeny bite.

We dip our fingers into the creamy frosting while Frijolito's back is turned.

On the top of my cake stands an elaborate plastic ballerina.

It wasn't my choice for the cake topper.

Mamy chose it.

I don't even like ballet.

I will never be an Alicia Alonso, the ballet hero of Cuba.

The positions we must memorize feel awkward and stiff, unlike Lu's dancing.

When Lu dances, her whole body moves like a wave over the ocean.

It is fluid and hypnotic.

I go to ballet class after school on Tuesdays.

It's awful.

Mamy makes me go.

There is a heavy girl next to me who pees or farts whenever she does her plies.

Then when she twirls, I get sprinkled on or the smell of urine wafts over, and I want to puke.

The only good thing about going to dance class is that we go to *El Carmelo*, the ice cream store across the street, when it is over.

That almost makes enduring the chubby, gassy ballerina worth it ... almost.

At 11:00, guests start to arrive.

I stand in the front of the house to greet my guests.

My friends file in along with their parents.

Some also have their *manejadoras*.

Lu is helping get the games ready in the patio.

She has made a treasure hunt and is writing clues on scraps of
  paper, which we need to find.

My brother finds the first clue and wins toy soldiers.

I am elated!

I find the next one, and I choose some gum.

Finally, it's time for the cake.

We all gather around and begin to sing "Appy BirDAY to you."

We proudly sing the whole song in English.

I make a wish and blow out all my candles before all the wax spills
  onto the cake.

Tied to the ballerina is a hidden candy.

When the cake is cut, whoever gets the piece with the candy also
  gets to keep the ballerina and pick a prize.

I hope I win the *rifa*, but it is always my lucky cousin Yoly who
  takes home the raffle prizes every time.

Today, she keeps her winning streak alive and will get to keep the
  dancer.

She also gets some dominoes as her prize.

Next we eat.

I am happy — since it is my birthday, I get to sit next to cousin
  Tensy.

All of us girls always fight to sit next to her.

She is the oldest girl, and she is gorgeous.

After we play and take pictures, it is time for my friends to leave.

Mamy and Papy say goodbye to the parents and I thank them for
  coming.

Now it is just us.
I tear open the paper and untie the bows on all the presents.
Lu is here.
She collects the wrappings to throw away but keeps the pretty
ribbons.
I smile and laugh.
I am surrounded by family.
Life is good.

After I unwrap the last gift, I go upstairs and spot an envelope on
my pillow.
I hastily tear it open. Inside I see a beautiful drawing of a bunny.
Lu knows bunnies are my favorite, and she remembers that I adore
her sketches.
She signs it, *Happy Birthday, mi niña. Love, your Lu.*

I love Lu so very much!

CUBY'S FIRST BIRTHDAY

Chapter 17

Spilled Sandwiches

"Hurry, Iluminada!" Señora Cubita's voice reaches my ears. I am outside putting the finishing touches on the tables. I fold the final napkins, push in the chairs so they are all straight, then head inside. Birthdays are special days in the house. I want to help make it a magical time for my Conga. I have already made the cherry Jell-O, making sure to add grapes just the way Conga likes it. It is setting in the refrigerator. I mix the deviled ham, pickles, and the cream cheese. I am making the *bocaditos*. I am sure to cut the crust off of the American *pan de molde*. I assemble the ham mixture and spoon it onto the white bread. After I cut them diagonally and place an olive slice on top to adorn them, I arrange them unto the silver tray. The secret to keeping them moist is to place a thin wet cheesecloth between the layers of sandwiches.

I don't have long. The party will begin shortly. Time is not my friend. There still so much to do. I tell Conga to put her dress on. She gives me her face. "Just put it on to please your mother," I tell her. When she leaves, I put a special card for her on her pillow. I am so happy to have her in my life. She is an amazing girl. We share the same spirit. I feel we have a special connection.

I hurry Conga downstairs and finish making hints to the treasure game. I have made it a little more difficult than in years past. The children are getting smarter and faster! Guests are due to arrive any minute. I grab the tray of *bocaditos* and open the door to the patio. Tulito comes in barreling through the doorway. He charges right into me, running at full speed, and down go all the tasty triangles. The entire tray of sandwiches are strewn about the tile floor. "Sorry!" he says, barely decreasing the speed at which he is running down the hall. Dulce sits on a chair outside. She takes note of what happened but doesn't scold him. She doesn't lift a finger to help me clean up the mess either. Of all the people who work in the house, she is the only one whose company I do not care to keep.

I quickly gather the sandwiches, throw them away, remake them, and get them on the table just as the first guests arrive. It will be a long day, but the smile on Conga's face makes it all worthwhile. She is a ball of happiness.

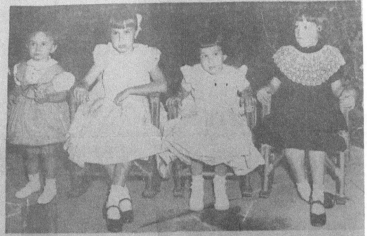

Irene Argote y Chacón, Tensy Silva Alvarez, Cubita Pérez Silva, la festejada; y Carmenchu Errotaberea Silva, en la fiesta infantil de ayer.

Fiesta infantil a Cubita Pérez Silva

En ocasión de cumplir cinco años la encantadora e inteligente niña Cubita Pérez Silva, hija muy querida del doctor René Pérez Amargós, prestigioso juez de Regla la Grande, y de su bella esposa, señora Cuba Silva,

en horas de la tarde de ayer, sábado, le fué ofrecida una fiesta infantil en la magnifica residencia que tienen en "Faubourg" de la Víbora pueden sus abuelos paternos, el doctor Delio Silva, presidente del Tribunal Superior y su gentilísima esposa, señora Cuba Herrera.

Fué un evento encantador que comenzó a las cuatro de la tarde y se prolongó hasta siete, en la más sana y conti la alegría, brincando al compás Argoles allí reunidos todos gozaron de veras y experimentaron una incógnita asistencia obsequiada.

Con la fotografía de vista que Pérez Silva, se reunieron siguientes niños:

Irene Argote y Chacón

CONGA SITTING NEXT TO TENSY

Silvia Fernández Macnamara, María Cristina Pellicier Chacón, Rosa Pérez Silva, Chelo Andreu Muñoz y Pat Gandrada Silva, que asistieron a la fiesta de Cubita Pérez Silva.

Fiesta infantil a Cubita Pérez Silva...

(Continuación de la página C-2)

niños y Tony Silva Alvarez, hija...

YOLY THE RIFA WINNER

69

Chapter 18

La Finca

I wake up early because I am so excited to get there.

I look out from the balcony and can still see the early morning fog covering the park.

It is Thursday, but we have no school for *Semana Santa* — the Easter holiday.

"*Vamos!*" I say as I tug on Mamy's nightgown. "Let's go to the farm!"

Long weekends are usually spent either at our beach house in Tarara, or at *la finca*, our farm.

Years ago, my *Abuelo* bought a huge parcel of land called *La Juanita*.

We simply call it *La Finca*.

It lies in the outskirts of Havana.

All the family enjoys it.

The fresh air, the animals, the family, and the FREEDOM!

He made sure the house there had plenty of room for everyone.

He gave all his children's families a bedroom in each corner, leaving the middle area for the living room and spending time together.

At the *finca*, the four of us sleep in the same bedroom, but there is just too much to do outside.

We are rarely in our room.

Once we get there, all the kids get to go wherever they want.
We are left to play until the frogs begin to croak and the darkness
    overtakes the light.

After about a thirty-minute drive, I can see the tops of the pines
    that line the long driveway.
The air smells different than it does at home.
We are almost there.

I see the three black and white cows.
One is named Chucha, one Cubita (my Mamy), and one Yolanda.
They are large and gentle.
I think they provide us with milk.
I don't really know.
I don't like milk unless it is in my coffee.

The car stops.
We are greeted by Pito, my chicken.
Every year around Lent we go to Woolworths.
Outside there is a woman selling chicks.
They are not ordinary chicks.
They are chicks dyed every color of the rainbow.
All the cousins get to pick one to take home.
I grab the blue one.
My brother chooses green, Carmenchu pink, Renecito orange,
    Tulito red, and Yoly the only yellow one.
Tensy never gets one.
She hates feathers.
They all usually die in just a matter of days.
My Pito was the only one that lived past Easter last year.

We brought him to the farm.

He is a lovable chicken who thinks he is a dog.

As soon as a car appears in the driveway, Pito is the first to greet you.

I scoop Pito up, give him a kiss, then run to the pen to see my pet
goat.

I named him Little Lamb.

Santa brought me a lamb for Christmas.

When I first got him, he was a baby.

Lu and I had to feed him with a baby bottle.

First he lived with us in CARDECUYOTU.

I loved bringing him to the park across the street, and he would
come when I called him.

Soon, Abuela did not like the idea of Little Lamb in the house, so
we had to bring him to the *finca*.

He is much wilder now and not very small.

He has long sharp horns and has been known to buck people, but
he is still always sweet to me.

I love him so.

We are the first ones to arrive, but in a matter of minutes the dust
on the driveway stirs and my aunts, uncles, and all the cousins
pull in.

Yes! They are here!!

They park their cars and get out.

I look down and suddenly realize Little Lamb is not at my side.

I glance up to see her charging for my aunts.

They are screaming and running around like angry ants when you
step on their hill.

My mother is crying.

Yolanda finds the closest tree, a large *guayaba*, and scoots up as high as she can.

Olga is close behind her, hanging on for her life.

Of all the trees around, she decides to climb the same one as Yolanda.

Olga is safe now.

Next, it is Mamy who is sprinting from my pet.

Even though the yard is filled with trees, the cars are close by, and the house is near, she goes for the *guayaba* tree and joins the others.

Finally, poor Aunt Chucha in her panicked state isn't thinking.

"Why is she going to the same tree?" I say to myself.

Chucha is the slowest but finally makes it to the tree.

Their butts are nearly in each other's faces as they scramble to get higher.

"Climb!" Chucha screams. "CLIMB!"

They are shrieking and screaming for help.

Chucha is the last one on.

Little Lamb is charging fast and Chucha's rear is a good shaped target.

She will be gored in seconds.

Just before impact, the farmer comes.

He grabs Little Lamb by the horns just like a Spanish matador.

He leads him away and back to his pen.

All of us kids are rolling on the floor laughing at our mothers up in a tree.

The men are roaring hysterically.

Uncle Tony's laugh booms.

He has the greatest laugh in the world.

They laugh so hard tears stream from their eyes and fall to the dirt.

They call the women *comemierdas* (fools) for all trying to climb the same tree.

The women are shaking and in shock.

Yolanda shakes her head and shows her disappointment that the men were of no help.

I hear swearing and laughing.

They finally scramble down as soon as Little Lamb is out of sight.

They go inside.

I think Olga faints.

Lu hurries inside and brings them lemonade.

That was enough excitement for the adults, but for us the fun is just beginning.

We pile into the cart that Abuelo had made for us.

The cart is pulled by Rocinante, named after Don Quijote's horse.

But he is far from the real Rocinante.

He is an old black mare that doesn't even like to trot.

He is our slow but steady taxi that brings us to all our frequented spots in the countryside.

Chuchin takes the reins, and we are off to explore.

First, we take the cart to see Sylvana and Carlota.

They are the massive boars that belong to me and my brother.

"Who wants to play Bridge of Death?" says Renecito.

It is unanimous – everyone agrees to play.

I am the second to go.

I step on the thin wooden gate which connects to the stone wall that separates the boars from the cacti on the other side.

I pretend I am in the circus and step as carefully and as gracefully as a tight rope walker.

The boars are noisy with large scary tusks, and the sty is putrid.

I know that one false move and I either end up plastered in the stinking red mud running from the pigs or covered with cactus needles imbedded into my skin.

It is terrifying for me to think of either consequence.

I carefully put my foot down and one of the stones dislodges. It falls to the ground quickly disappearing under the festering sludge.

I lose my balance, falter, and think "This is it."

Out of nowhere I look up to see my brother's outstretched hand.

I manage to grab it before I fall.

He holds me tight and yanks me forward.

Victory is mine!

I have prevailed!

I have crossed the Bridge of Death!

My cousins clap and cheer.

After all of us safely make it across, we pile back into the cart.

Andale, Rocinante!

EL→PILLO

RENECITO

NEAR THE BRIDGE OF DEATH

ALL THE COUSINS WITH ABUELO & ABUELA

Chapter 19

La Finca and Tormenta

It is a pleasant spring morning and the family is preparing to go to *la finca* for the weekend. I am happy to join them. Tasty meals, laughter, adventures, and games await. The entire Silva clan is getting together for a weekend of merriment. Conga tells me it is one of her favorite places in the world. I finish packing the car with all the essentials and throw in some jump ropes. The girls love to jump rope on the driveway and the boys pretend they are real *vaqueros* with the ropes. A caravan of cars leave CARDECUYOTU.

Conga has been singing "I'm a Yankee Doodle Dandy" all morning, pretending she is riding a pony. She is dressed in her cowgirl outfit. I myself have never been on a horse. Their enormous size scares me.

There is such freedom at *la finca*. The children are allowed to do as they please. They are really quite well behaved, but sometimes they like to play pranks on the adults and each other. It is just my luck that today the biggest prankster of them all is here, their

77

cousin El Pillo. He is a rascal-always joking around. I had no idea today was going to be my day. Renecito and Neny are riding their horses around the pigs' corral. The girls are teasing the pigs, Carlota and Sylvana. I am watching them and loving life. El Pillo and Chuchin approach me. I should have known I was in trouble. They dare me to ride Tormenta. They say he is the wildest stallion of all. Conga overhears and tells them "Lu is always ready for a challenge. Of course she will ride."

I do feel that I am up for the task. I'm very limber, fit, and quite fearless. I decide I will ride Tormenta. We must grab life by the horns sometimes! Chuchin steadies him and El Pillo gives me a lift. As I am still trying to sit on the saddle, he takes off. I am soon a crying mess, scared and yelling at the top of my lungs, trying to stop him. After a violent ride, he throws me off. I can't get up. My leg feels broken. Bright red blood comes gushing out of the wound. Señora Cuba runs over to help me. I have hardly ever seen her outside and definitely have never seen her run. This must be bad. Conga is sobbing and the boys disappear quickly. My leg is mended. I will live. But never will I mount a horse again. Not even a pony called Macaroni.

FUN AT THE FINCA

← ROCINANTE AND OUR CART

Chapter 20

Radio Reloj da la Hora

All the cousins have horses at the *finca*.
Chuchin had to have the biggest and strongest.
He named him Tormenta.
Tormenta is mean and wild.
He is hard to control and difficult to ride.
Once El Pillo and Chuchin dared Lu into riding him, and Tormenta
    bucked her off and kicked her as she fell.
She never even got in the saddle.
Her leg was bloodied and looked pretty bad.
I was relieved to see that she didn't get any horrible injuries.
I never saw any bruises.
Later I realized she must have been covered in bruises, but her skin
    was too dark for them to show.
I brought her some Vicks VapoRub.
Mamy said she doesn't know what they put in that tiny blue
    container, but it is like magic.
It always helped us feel better.

Renecito's horse is named Belleza.
She is big, brown, and very tame.
Yoly's is smaller and called Bellezita.
She is Belleza's offspring.
Azabache is my brother's stallion.
Everyone knows he is the best.

He is a jet-black beauty.

My horse is Azabachito.

He is lovable and small.

Carmenchu, Cuquito, Tensy, and Tonito do not have their own horses, but there are always plenty to ride.

Tensy, Carmenchu, and I braid their manes and brush them till they are silky and smooth.

We ride them around the pastures, and the boys practice lassoing.

We play cops and robbers, which we change into a version of hide-and-seek.

The girls don't really want to play.

"We will only play if we can hide first," Carmenchu says.

"OK … ready, go!" says Cuquito, her brother.

We all hide.

There are so many great spots.

I crouch behind the outhouse.

It smells, but I am sure to win.

No one comes around here.

Only the farmer uses it.

It works.

I win.

I am the last to be caught by the boy cops.

"OK, our turn to hide," says Renecito.

"Nah, we don't want to play anymore," Carmenchu says.

They angrily chase us, but we run inside for protection from our parents.

Later, my brother fills me in on his plan.

He tells me that as soon as we arrived, he had found an old glass bottle and a cork that fit it perfectly.

He decided that every time he farted, he would hold the bottle up
to his butt and capture the gas in the bottle.
He has been carrying it around all weekend. Wherever he is, that
bottle is with him.

We are up in the *guayaba* trees.
Boys are the captains and girls are the stewardesses.
We play in the leaves, lost in our imaginations for hours.
My brother tells us to stay in the trees, and we will be safe.
He is ready to unveil his masterpiece.
He climbs down the trunk and walks by my father, bottle in hand.
Papy says to him, "What do you have there? I have been watching
you walk around forever carrying that bottle!"
"Come look!" Neny says.
As soon as my father gets his nose millimeters from the bottle, my
brother removes the cork and the foul aroma of finely aged farts
pours out of the bottle and infiltrates all the surrounding air.
It is almost enough to knock my father to the ground.
I have never seen Neny run so fast.

In the afternoon we huddle around the radio.
We have no television at the *finca*.
It is Good Friday, so we listen to the Stations of the Cross on the
radio.
It takes hours.
We listen as the radio voice explains in detail every step Jesus took
along the *Via Dolorosa* — the path Jesus took to his crucifixion.
After each line read my aunts and Mamy are *llorando a moco
tendido* — crying their brains out.
They shake and sniffle so much it seems as if they are each trying
to outdo each other.

Yoly smirks at me, and my smile almost turns to a giggle.

But before a chuckle emerges, Yolanda glares at me with the evil eye reminding me to be silent and serious.

Although I feel extremely guilty, I wish it would just hurry and get to the part where Jesus dies, so the radio show would end, and we could get outside and play.

After at least another hour, it is over.

Papy turns the knob of the radio.

The women are somber.

The husbands hand them their white handkerchiefs to wipe their eyes and noses.

They take their rosaries out and pray some more.

The men sit and talk.

The kids rush outside and run, laugh, and let loose.

It's not easy to sit there silent for so long.

The bathroom in the *finca* is pretty big.

It has a shower and multiple sinks, and it is long and spacious.

The wall of the bathroom doesn't fully connect to the ceiling, so you can hear if someone is singing in the shower or see the steam trickling over the wall if you are in the living room.

After showering, Tensy, Carmenchu, and Yoly wrap themselves in towels and sit in the bathroom painting their nails.

It's my chance to shower.

I turn the water on and start to hum.

Today the boys decide to play a trick on us.

They have collected jars of frogs and have been planning a secret attack.

They wait for the right moment to release them.

They toss them over the wall and into the bathroom full of us girls.

As I go to adjust the angle of the water spout, I look up and see a frog.
A FLYING frog.
It lands next to me with a plop on the wet tile.
Moments later, I hear a series of ear-piercing shrieks.
I peek out around the shower curtain and see at least ten more
    frogs jumping around the bathroom.
One even jumps into the white terry turban on top of Tensy's head.
All the girls grab their towels to cover up and race out of the
    bathroom.
There are no towels left.
But I run out after them.
I use my hands to cover my breasts, which are not even buds.
From the waist up, I am as flat as Lu's ironing board.
I look up and all the boys are there.
They point at me and laugh.
I soon realize that I am covering my chest, but my papaya is there
    for all to see.
I retreat to the bathroom.
I'd rather be with the frogs.
Lu comes in with clothes and helps console me.
"I will get them," I say.
"I know you will, Conga. I know you will."

It is still dark, but I hear the rooster calling me — *quiquiriquí!*
I am awake but it is just me.
I walk to the living room and sit on the sofa wondering who will
    be the next one up, and what we will get into today.
I walk to the kitchen and see the clock: 6:16 a.m.
In Havana, we listen to a radio station called *Radio Reloj.*
It only gives news and updates, but every single minute it states
    the time.

I spy an enormous black spider inching across the wall and I know just what to do.

I decide that I will become the *Radio Reloj* announcer this morning.

"*Radio Reloj da la hora:* The time is 6:17 a.m. There is a spider on the wall."

"*Radio Reloj da la hora:* The time is 6:18 a.m. The spider is on the move."

"*Radio Reloj da la hora:* The time is 6:19 a.m. The spider is climbing closer to Yolanda's room."

I carry on this way, loudly announcing the time and giving updates on the spider every minute for nearly ten minutes.

I hear grumbling coming from the bedrooms ....

"Cállate!"

"Shut up, Cuby!"

"Coño!"

They yell, but no one has surfaced.

They don't believe me.

"*Radio Reloj da la hora:* The time is 6:20 a.m.: The spider is about to enter Yolanda's room."

Finally, a few adults all angry and groggy emerge from their corner rooms.

I hear a collective shriek.

The entire house is up now.

The giant spider is as big as my hand.

There is pure terror on Mamy's face.

I think Olga faints again.

It is a tarantula.

A big, hairy, black tarantula.

The boys grab brooms to try to steer it outside, using the handle.

The gigantic spider squeezes under the door. It tries to disappear
into the dark morning.

With Lu by my side, I am brave.

We try to follow it, but we lose sight of the creature as it shuffles
under the leaves.

I wanted to catch it and throw it over the wall when the boys were
taking their showers, but it escaped me.

I may be one of the smallest and youngest of the cousins, but it
doesn't matter.

My confidence makes up for my size.

I am happy enough that I woke the boys up so early.

They are always the last to emerge.

They are tired and grumpy.

Lu and I give up the hunt and decide to pick bananas instead.

Lu shows me the ones that are the best.

She can tell by their smell, their color, and by the way they feel.

We gather a few that are small, ripe, and ready to eat.

All the cousins call a truce at breakfast.

My brother puts his cowboy costume on.

We run outside.

The Lone Ranger needs our help.

NENY, CHUCHIN, RENECITO
TULITO, YOLY, TENSY, CARMEN, CUBY

YOLANDA, MAMY, MANUEL — MY BISABUELO, ABUELO &
THE COUSINS

Chapter 21

Wednesday Night

Wednesday nights are my favorites.

Mamy always lets me help her pick out the jewelry she will wear.

She loves jewelry.

Her gold bangles, wedding ring, and diamond solitaire never leave
her body.

For her birthday every year, she would choose a ring or a piece with
a precious gem that Papy would buy her.

Today I choose an aquamarine ring for her to wear to go with her
pearls.

She always wears high heels.

Her closet is full of them.

Papy usually wears his guayaberas.

Often, my Aunt Yolanda and Uncle René join them along with
Olga and Tony and one or two other couples.

Sometimes they go to the *Tropicana*.

They have dancing shows, dinner, and gambling there.

Papy says it is never wise to gamble.

They eat out at many different restaurants in the city.

Sometimes they go to the movies.

Whenever they tell us they are going to the cinema, I tell Mamy not
to forget to bring me back some chocolate cigarettes.

I love them.

Lu laughs as I dance around the house and sing *"Fumando espero
al hombre que yo quiero"* in my best Sarita Montiel voice, as
I hold the candy to my lips.
Sometimes Mamy and Papy and their friends attend canasta
parties.
The couples alternate hosting the parties at their homes.

I love Wednesday nights, because I get to spend more time with Lu.
Today she is making bonito sandwiches for the adults.
It is Mamy and Papy's turn to host canasta here, so Lu prepares
many delicious appetizers.
She lets Neny and me try each one before they are served.
I tell her the tiny bonito fish sandwiches with the olives on top are
the best, but everything tastes so good.

After Lu serves the food, we head to our bedroom and play
Parcheesi.
I never win, but I always have fun.
I pretend with the chocolate cigarettes that I'm a star, but I'm
actually very happy no one in my family smokes cigarettes.
Que asco!

The smell of cigarettes makes my stomach turn.

MAMY

Our night at... TROPICANA

HAVANA'S FABULOUS NIGHT CLUB & CASINO

PAPY

LOLITA ARARA... "CANASTA PARTY" OFRE(

CUBA

HNC

1930

Foto SOUVENIR de

"Templete" Restaurant

Ave. del PUERTO AND NARCISO LOPEZ STREET

M-4087   M-5284

Chapter 22

The Solares

Mamy is out shopping downtown.

"She's gone!" I scream.

We go out the back door and climb the black iron spiral stairs that lead to Lu's apartment.

I open the door to the small upstairs living space.

I'm greeted with *criollo*, *sofrito*, and other exotic smells.

It seemed there was always food cooking from the morning's *café con leche* and *pan Cubano* to the evening's red snapper and *potaje*.

I go to her dresser and look through her vanity.

I admire her small collection of beauty products.

Lu takes the handkerchief out and sets her hair free.

It is frizzy and black.

She takes out an iron and turns on music while it heats up.

She takes it to her hair.

It is transformed.

It is shiny, black, and longer than before.

It is like magic. She is so, so beautiful!

While she finishes her hair, I sit on the roof and watch the neighborhood from above.

She calls me inside and asks me to help her pick out a dress.

She gives me advice on how to dress, but I am not into fashion, so I don't pay attention until she says, "Black girls never wear green, because it makes us look like a steak with parsley."

I laugh.

I am tan, and I would look more like a chicken with parsley, I think.

I decide I will stay away from green dresses anyway.

She models a few choices.

They are simple but pretty.

I like the red one with tiny yellow flowers.

She agrees it looks good.

She will wear it on her day off Sunday.

She is going to Matanzas to see her family.

She changes back into her uniform.

She is ready, and we head out.

She takes my hand and we walk a while, then down an alley — until we are at the forbidden *solares*.

There is music.

There is color.

There is life.

There are half-naked black babies toddling around.

There are women sitting on wooden boxes near the street.

Some of the *solares* are tall buildings

Others are small, one-story homes that house many different families.

They all face the alley.

Many families share a living space, like labyrinths with hidden passages and huge columns.

I don't have friends here, but I always find someone to play with when I come.

I see statues of saints in the doorsteps.
I ask Lu about them, and she tells me Santería shares some ideas
     with Catholicism.
People who practice Santería don't go to a church though.
They have ceremonies at home or in public places.
There is one area in our park under the big tree where I have seen
     apples wrapped in purple cloths, coins, and offerings.
I once saw a headless pigeon with coins and feathers.
I don't like to go to that corner without Lu.
It scares me.

Some houses have altars filled with *pasteles*, cookies, gold coins,
     and fruit with candles burning.
Lu says these are offerings to their *orisha*, who is a spiritual guide
     in Santería.
I smell rum and cigars.
Through windows, I see people all dressed in white.
Lu tells me they are being initiated into the religion.
Lu always has answers to all of my questions.
She has heard they cannot leave their houses or touch anyone except
     their family members for over a year during the initiation.
I don't think I would like to do that.

Lu talks to some people she knows.
She helps braid some hair.
I love to come to this other world that seems so different, but so
     familiar.

It is forbidden by Mamy.
She knew I had come to the *solares* once and was furious.
It doesn't stop us.

We don't come often, but when we do, I love it.
It is mysterious.
It is enchanting.
It is mystical.
"Conga," Lu says, "Time to go. We must beat your mother home."
I round the corner and see our Hudson charging towards the
    house.
We race towards home and steal in the back.

"Señora Cubita, what would you like for me to prepare for dinner
    tonight?" Lu asks, still panting.
"How about *bistec*?" Mamy replies.

"With parsley," Lu adds giving me a wink.

SANTERÍA

Chapter 23

Tarara

It is a beautiful summer day, and we are headed to our beach house
in Tarara for the weekend.

Our green Hudson is a sturdy reliable car.

It also has a special feature.

On the floor in back, there is a hole that leads to the outside.

The hole isn't too large.

"I have to pee," Neny says.

We have just begun our trip and have thirty more minutes until
we arrive.

My father is driving and does not want to stop.

"Use the hole!" he says.

Neny lifts the floor mat to reveal the hole.

He quickly relieves himself and covers it back up.

I am sitting next to him and don't want to see.

I stare out the window.

We pass many cows.

I count at least twenty.

Sharing the road with us is a horse hooked up to a buggy with
other kids in it.

Our Hudson passes them quickly.

"Are you finished yet?" I ask.

"*Sí, pero* next I have to make a turd," he says with a sly grin.

He pretends to settle his butt on the hole.

"*Eres asqueroso*," I say.
My brother is disgusting.
Mamy tells him to stop.
He sits back down on the seat next to me and reads his comics.
We are almost there.

I smell the freshly cut grass.
I feel the salty air.
I love the beach.
I don't even go inside.
I head straight for the shore.
It is a short two blocks.
In our community, there are other houses with nice yards.
There are not too many people around today.
The water is clear and refreshing.
I watch the silver minnows swim around my toes.
Mamy is soon on the sand under an umbrella.
She hands me a Coca-Cola.
The bottle is covered in tiny water droplets.
It is sweating as much as Neny, who plops onto the sand next to me.
I drink every last drop, then the ocean calls me back.
When we return to the house, I see the Dodge.
My cousins Yoly and Renecito are here.
I go around back to the picnic table.
Lu has made sandwiches for lunch.
I take my pickles out and give them to Yoly.
She eyes my sandwich to see if I will finish it.
I give her the last few bites.
After lunch, the games begin.
We play London Bridge.
Next, we play basketball.

The boys all think they are Wilt Chamberlain.
Mamy made sure the hoop in the back wasn't too high.
None of us are very tall, and she likes us to score.

We make up all kinds of competitions.
Who can stand on one foot the longest?
Renecito.
Who can make it to the porch only stepping on leaves?
Neny.
Who can Hula-Hoop the longest?
Me!
The hoop spins around my waist.
I can make it go fast or slow.
I can walk with it, jump with it, and dance with it.
It never falls.
The others grow tired of watching me, so I let it fall gently onto
    the ground.
We start telling jokes, and as usual Yoly laughs so hard she pees
    her pants.
Night falls.
The warm breeze blows as the palm fronds dance in the wind, and
    I fall asleep counting stars.

After a few days, we are even browner, and almost ready to join the
    Harlem Globetrotters.
It's time to go back to La Víbora.
We pack up and load the car.
"Don't forget to use the bathroom!" I scream to Neny from the car.

Just in case, I scribble the words "OUT OF ORDER" onto a piece
    of scrap paper and post my sign on top of the hole.

TIBURÓN AT TARARA

CARMENCHU, TENSY, CUQUITO, CHUCHIN

99

HUDSON WITH THE "BATHROOM"

Chapter 24

La Víbora

Our neighborhood is called La Víbora.

It is the best.

Our neighborhood has everything.

You can walk everywhere.

I like it so much better than crowded downtown Havana, filled
with busy stores and towering buildings.

It is nicer than El Vedado, where you have to drive everywhere in
crowded three-lane highways.

I don't like El Miramar either, with its stuffy ornate gated
mansions.

I bet you never even see your neighbors there.

La Víbora has it all.

Our mansions are open with meticulous lawns.

We have smaller homes with perfectly swept patios.

It has the corner bodegas, the grocery stores, and the corner
farmacia for medicines.

It is filled with churches and schools.

On one corner sits the beauty parlor for the ladies and the
barbershop for the men.

We have a local tavern, *El Capitolio*, where you would be sure to
find my Uncle Tulio if you needed him.

You can see the *solares* and the parks.

The sidewalks have small hills that are perfect for our bikes and
  roller skates.

It is a safe place where everyone meets and plays freely.

La Víbora also has small variety stores, *quincallas*, which are my
  favorite.

I go in and lose track of time there.

After hours, I come out with a Bazooka bubblegum and my
  colorful *pirulí* pop.

I love to read the funny comic inside the gum wrapper, and
  everyone who sees me is jealous of my *pirulí*.

They are every kid's dream.

I put my skates back on and zoom down the hill blowing huge
  pink bubbles.

I stash my *pirulí* in my pocket for later.

I don't notice the stick in the sidewalk.

I try to maneuver around it but lose my balance and skid across
  the cement.

Lucky for me, La Víbora also has the *socorro*, the first aid clinic,
  where you go for emergencies.

After the fall, I struggle to get up.

My leg is bleeding and skin is hanging off my knee.

Neny bikes home and gets Mamy.

She takes me to the clinic.

They bandage me up and tell me to rest for a while.

Nothing is broken but my ego.

La Víbora is home to so many!

Everyone in Abuelo's family has moved here.

Abuelo's brother Aristides' family lives on Vista Alegre, the corner
   street.
Aristides' son, El Pillo, is always around, but he is older and mostly
   hangs out with Chuchin.
Anibal and Elida, Abuelo's other siblings, all live minutes away.
My Uncle René's family lives in the house behind us.
Uncle Cuco's family is down the block.
Nena, Tulito's mom, lives on Figueroa on the other side of Santa
   Catalina, just a few blocks walk away.
Olga, Tony, and Tonito are right in the neighborhood, too.
There's always a familiar face.

Today Mamy takes us to one of the small luncheonettes called *El
   Niagara.*
Food always helps us feel better.
I order a tasty Cuban sandwich.
My mother always gets an Elena Ruth or a *Medianoche* sandwich.
Neny orders the *fritas* and a *perro caliente.*
The hamburgers and hot dogs are better than anywhere.

I unwrap my *piruli* and savor the flavor of each color.
Mamy says we can go buy another, because of my injury.

My skinned knee is a small price to pay for more deliciousness.

LA VIBORA-OUR NEIGHBORHOOD

Chapter 25

Chit-Chat

As part of a household, you discover secrets. I go about my daily chores, trying to ignore the comments I hear. I go forward, doing what is asked of me to the best of my ability, caring for the loving children who have been entrusted to me. I see and hear a lot, some good, some bad, and some things I can't wait to share with my friends who work in the house with me. Many evenings we meet at the park to sit, relax, and chat.

Last night Fela had us in stitches as she described the next-door neighbor, Mrs. Saldaña, walking out in the early afternoon wearing her beige dress with a lace collar. She thought she looked so good! However, she must have forgotten to wear her girdle. There was a lot of shaking going on. We laughed and laughed, as Fela, who does not have an ounce of fat on her derrière, tried to imitate her jiggly walk. She told me Mrs. Saldana was jiggling more than the Jell-O we make for the kids. I laugh so hard I nearly fall off the bench. Berta, always the bearer of unpleasant news, announced that sweet Maria Isabel, who

works for the Hernandez household down the
block, was terminated. There is talk that Mr.
Hernandez got a bit too close to her. Without
favorable references it will be hard for her
to find new employment. My heart goes to her.
I feel fortunate working for the Silvas.

SILVIA

Chapter 26

Stars and Stripes Forever

My brother's school is very close to our house.
It is only for boys.
He is happy because he is in the older grades and gets to wear
    pants, not shorts, for his uniform.
My cousins Chuchin, Renecito, Tulito, Cuquito, and my brother all
    walk to school together. Renecito is always anxious at school.
He chews the end of his tie when he is nervous.
We laugh because by the time he gets home, half his tie is missing.
I bet my Aunt Yolanda gets tired of buying new ones.

I like going to school, but I do not like my uniform.
It consists of a white blouse with puffy sleeves and a black pleated
    skirt with black suspenders.
It is so uncomfortable.
Mamy reminds Lu to make it extra stiff.
She starches it three times at least.
My mother inspects and agrees it looks respectable.
God forbid I have any wrinkles.

After Mamy leaves, Lu tells me to take off my blouse. We rinse it
    with water.
The starch rinses away.
She dries it as best she can. I put it on.
It's still damp, but at least it does not feel like a scratchy brick.

I thank Lu with a hug and Pancho picks me up on bus number 10.

It is a short drive to my new school, the American Dominican Academy in El Vedado.

My school is filled with Cuban girls who are taught by American nuns.

It is a Catholic school.

We start each day with an assembly in the courtyard.

The nuns turn on music from America.

I think it is from the composer named Souza.

We march around with smiles.

It feels like we are in a New York City parade.

Next comes an announcement through the megaphone that we need to get to our first class.

Some girls stay at the school, but I go home every day from 11:00 to 2:00 for lunch and a siesta.

My favorite thing about school is recess time.

We play hopscotch and jump rope.

I like to buy a Coke from the vending machine.

I don't think any other schools have a vending machine.

I know Neny is jealous.

We play all sorts of fun games with the soda bottles, like Desde Córdoba a Sevilla, at recess, too.

Next, we go to the chapel and pray ....

I learn a bit of English at my school.

My parents want us to learn English.

I do not want to get to the sixth grade, though.

I hear everything is taught in English then.

We are so scared — especially Carmenchu, who is closer to sixth grade than me!

When I get home, I teach Lu her daily lesson, but she is not learning
    English that quickly.
She tells me "*no se le pega.*"
It just doesn't stick.
Either she is a poor student, or I am a bad teacher.
I start to hum the song from the morning assembly.
Lu picks up a spoon that becomes her baton, and we begin to
    march all around the house.

"Stars and Stripes Forever."

FIRST DAY OF SCHOOL

Chapter 27

Venceremos

I call my brother René "Neny."

Neny is smart and amusing.

We may fight sometimes, but we usually do have a lot of fun together.

We are exactly 15 months apart in age.

Even though I only have one sibling, I feel like I have eight.

The cousins do everything together.

I love them all equally, with a fierce feeling of togetherness.

Chuchin is the leader: He is the oldest, and whatever he says is the law.

Tensy is our cherished one: We just live to be near her, and she can do no wrong.

Renecito is the prankster: The outlaw, the dangerous one.

Carmenchu is sweet, beautiful, and innocent: She is the epitome of a good girl, and she is my closest cousin.

Yoly is the funny one: She is outspoken; full of laughter, joy, and tricks; and is the inventor of fearless adventures.

Tulito is mysterious, an enigma: It's often hard to know what he is thinking, and he never takes the reins, but he never misses out on anything.

Cuquito is my sidekick: Times are always easy with him, and he is always there with me.

Neny, well what can I say?

He's my other half.

We live life through each other's eyes.
He is the brilliant one — the one that gets the Friday dollar from
    Abuelo Delio for bringing home the best weekly grades.

And me — I am always told that a light shines when I enter a room.
I am myself.
Who knows?

Carmenchu lives in CARDECUYOTU, too.
Her room is upstairs, like mine.
We are inseparable.
We spend day and night together.
Carmenchu likes the park, but she also loves to play inside.
Her brother Cuquito and Neny go outside to play baseball.
We get my box of paper dolls and hurry downstairs.
We use the entire hallway.
We build houses, stores, and places our dolls can go.
Carmenchu's nanny, Fela, is nice, but she often is too busy to play.

Lu sits with us on the cool marble and draws new dresses for our
    dolls.
We color them in with pencils and Carmenchu always adds great
    designs.
In our hallway, we make our version of the department store
    downtown, called *El Encanto*.
We move the dolls into the store.
They will try on the latest Lu fashions.
"Make sure you look out for bombs behind the toilets!" Carmenchu's
    doll says to mine.
We know that there is war brewing in Cuba, and our parents warn
    us of danger.

After going to the bathroom and not finding any bombs, my doll
   chooses a beautiful blue dress.
"Perfect fit!" I say.

Next, we take out my tea set and have a party.
Tensy joins us, and she knows just how to set the table.
We invite everyone to the party.
Lu has coffee in her cup instead of tea.
Some of the grownups may have rum.
I have tea with two cubes of sugar.
After our tea, Carmenchu goes back upstairs.
Her mother Chucha insists that she read.
Tensy goes home.
I walk outside and find Abuelo in his rocker.

Neny is back.
He grabs his marbles, and Chuchin comes out, too.
We sit on the porch, ready to play.
Neny keeps winning and collecting more and more marbles.
Out of nowhere there is a loud boom.
It sounds like a loud sharp crack of thunder.

We look up to see a man in a brown shirt staggering across the
   street and straight to our porch.
"*Ayudame! Por favor!!! Ayudame!*" he wails.
I look at his midsection and realize he is struggling to keep his
   intestines inside of his body.
The red spot on his uniform is spreading as blood seeps through
   and begins to drip on the steps.
His fingerless hands are desperately trying to push his guts back in.
Blood has soaked through and now covers most of his shirt.

My grandfather runs inside and makes a call.
An ambulance picks up the wounded man.
His color is faded.
He looks up and stares in our eyes.
"Patria o Muerte! Venceremos!"
Fatherland or death. We will win.
The bomb he was going to plant in the park prematurely went off
     in his hands.

The revolution is on our doorstep.

MY PAPERDOLLS

CUBY & CARMENCHU

Chapter 28

Churros

It is cold in Cuba.

It doesn't happen too often, but today the temperature dipped below 15 degrees C.

The teenagers pull out their flannel pink poodle skirts and I get my sweater out from the box in my closet.

I love when I can have an excuse to put my Chapstick on.

I smother my lips with the smooth wax.

It glides easily onto my lips.

I knock at Carmenchu and Cuquito's door.

Our house in December is magical.

A beautiful Christmas village is on display at my Aunt Chucha's every year.

How lovely and enchanting snow must be.

Cuquito and I make a fort out of bedsheets.

We call it our Christmas Club.

We talk about all things Christmas.

We exchange secrets about what we want to give our cousins, and we make our wish lists for Santa Claus.

One of the best things about the cold weather is that it brings the churro man to our street.

That's not to say I don't love the frozen slushy cart with its *granizados.*

The delightful colored syrups always entice us over.
There is also the man yelling, "peanuts, peanuts for sale!"
I am also fond of the Gallego from Spain, who wears a black
  beret and walks by our house selling the freshest and juiciest
  tangerines.
These are all amazing, but the churro man is special.
He sets up his cart right at the corner by our house.

"Please, Mamy, just one?" I beg.
She gives me five cents and I hurry out the door.
It's fascinating to see the dough being pushed through the holes
  of the machine.
Huge, white, spaghetti-looking noodles come pouring out.
The vendor cuts the long dough and puts it in a small stained fryer
  box.
He dips the dough into the burning oil.
It comes out crispy, golden, and perfectly warm.
I can hardly wait for him to sprinkle them with sugar and dust
  them with cinnamon.
Finally, he places them in a brown bag, and they are mine.
"*Gracias!*" I say, my mouth watering.
I happily make my way down the street.

I get to the park and hear whimpering.
A scared, brown mutt is shivering in the grass.
His amber eyes are sad.
A stray.

People would often leave unwanted puppies in the park, or
  sometimes the mother dog with no owner would have her
  litter on the upper part of the park near the field.

I look around and see no mother.

The small pup reminds me of my dog, Rin Tin Tin.

Papy's friend Manolo Vega, who lived in the country and had many animals, once gave me a small German Shepherd puppy.

Manolo Vega also gave us most of our animals at the farm: Our horse Azabache, our pigs Carlota and Sylvana, and many more.

I called my German Shepherd pup Rin Tin Tin.

We watched American TV, and I thought all the girl dogs were named Lassie and all the boy dogs were named Rin Tin Tin.

The first year of his life Rin Tin Tin became sick with parvo.

We would go visit him in the dog hospital, where I would pet him as he slept in his cage.

His passing left me very sad.

It was the first death of a loved one I ever experienced.

It is too cold for this puppy to be outside.

I give him the last bite of my churro and gather him in my cardigan sweater.

I sneak past Abuela's watchful eyes.

She always seems to know what is going on before it happens.

I run inside and find Lu.

Lu is a great accomplice.

We agree that the puppy must stay with us.

My heart belongs to the animals.

There is a talking parrot in the house next door — its cage is near my bedroom.

We always chat.

She is always my first morning call.

I also love monkeys.

Our family would vacation at *Isla de Pinos*, south of Havana in the
Golfo de Batabanó.

The ferry would take us there.

We would spend days living in cabins engulfed by nature, eating
mangoes hanging from the trees while swimming in ponds
with crystal-clear caves.

The island was filled with an abundance of monkeys and parrots.

Papy would promise me every time we went that I could take a
monkey home.

I loved the monkeys and desperately wanted one, but so far, my
dream has yet to come true.

I think my love of animals comes from my other *abuela*, Iraida,
whose small apartment in downtown Havana is always filled
with creatures of all kinds.

Her dog's name *Linda* means pretty, but she never lived up to her
name.

Linda would greet you at the door and stick her muzzle up under
your skirt or pants and in your crotch.

Mamy used to say if she couldn't get you when you arrived, she
would get you when you left.

Wild birds lived in Abuela Iraida's tiny front porch and various
cats would roam the open-air corridors of her humble home.

I am still sad about the pig that Frijolito had to kill for *Noche
Buena.*

We played with the pig in our back yard for hours the day before
Christmas Eve, right until it ended up with a knife in its throat.

Frijolito tried for so long to catch it.

The pig ran circles around him.

It went in, out, over, and under Frijolito's legs.

He was swearing, sweating, and raving mad.
He finally did catch him and ended up cooking him.
He gave a good fight.
I was really rooting for the pig.

Although my love of animals runs deep, Mamy has made it clear
    that no more animals are allowed in the house.
I have my rabbits.
They live in Papy's study in our house.
They have no cages but never leave the premises.
I never see poop or pee on the floor.
Lu must clean the marble floors many times daily.
Last week, Papy built them a huge hutch outside on our upstairs
    porch.
Lu loves animals almost as much as I do.
We have hidden several bunnies and other strays that have been
    discovered, so it is becoming harder to find new places to hide
    them.

We take the new puppy into the small storage room where Lu
    keeps her mops and brooms.
He stays warm from the heat of the oven that is behind it.
He is safe and cozy.

Maybe someday I will find a monkey.

SANTA, NUN, SHEPHERD, CUBY, JOSEPH, MARY, ANGEL, STAR, & A BIG BABY JESUS

CUBY CHRISTMAS PAGEANTS

Chapter 29

Sidra and Sadness

Noche Buena is the best day of the year.
The food is scrumptious.
Lechón asado and all the fixings, *congri*, and *yuca con mojo* are
    always on the menu.
There are also delicacies imported from Spain such as *turrones* —
    Jijona and *Alicante*, walnuts, hazelnuts, dates, and figs. We can
    only find them in the stores during the holidays.
They are a delectable treat.
Abuela's table is overflowing with every savory dish imaginable.
We stay up and have a late dinner.
Then in the morning — Santa Claus and Christmas.
La Navidad is always just perfect.

We are upstairs, and Lu has just finished helping me write my wish
    list to the *Reyes Magos*:

7, December 1958

My Dear Three Wise Men,
A kiss to each of you, and now I am going to tell you what I want
    you to bring me.
A little store like the one in the El Encanto catalogue. It is cheap:
    $4.65.

A stroller for my dolls.
A washing set with a pail, basket, and sink: $2.00.
A new dress, very pretty.
A little gold ring.
A tea set.
La muñeca, named Arthimise, a doll made out of felt and stuffed
    with candy: $2.95.
Kisses from Cuba Vivian Fabiola de Fátima.

It's time to celebrate!
Mamy and Papy have gone out for the night.
Lu is with her family in Matanzas.
All the cousins and Tonito are downstairs with Abuela and Abuelo.

New Year's Eve is also one of the best holidays.
We throw a bucket of water out the door at midnight to wash away
    all the evil things that had happened that year.
We eat 12 grapes, one for each month of the year, to give us luck.
We take a giant jump at midnight, so we are not left behind, but
    instead we hop into the New Year.

I hear the pop of champagne bottles, and even I get some sidra.
There is loud laughter, simple joy, smiles, and happiness.
We stay up past midnight for hours, dancing and playing.
My eyes are tired, but I want to stay up.
I close my eyes … I only need a few minutes of rest.
I am awakened by the sound of the telephone.
All the adults are still awake and enjoying themselves — I find
    I am still downstairs.
I have no idea what time it is, but Mamy and Papy are home now.

Being the President of the Supreme Court, my grandfather Delio
     is one of the first to receive the call.
His ear is on the receiver for less than ten seconds.
My grandfather puts the phone up.
"He is gone."
Batista has fled.
Abuelo's face lacks all emotion.
The music stops.
The laughs turn to gasps.
The men's boisterous jokes turn to solemn conversations.
Mamy and Yolanda begin to cry.
The party stopped.
Uncertainty knocked on our door.

Our Cuba was gone.

LETTER TO THE 3 WISE MEN

Chapter 30

Fidel Castro

I am headed back home for the holidays. I take the bus to see my family in Matanzas. I bring them gifts from the city.

It is 6:00 a.m. A new year is beginning – 1959. I hear my father's radio blaring. The newscaster announced that *El Comándante* Fidel Castro succeeded in overthrowing the troops of *el General* Fulgencio Batista, who has fled Cuba with his family. They boarded a plane to Santo Domingo in the early morning hours.

"Iluminada, come quickly. I want everyone together," my father says. I run and sit by his side. My mother and brothers are holding hands. Some of my neighbors left Matanzas a few years back to join the guerrillas. They went to the *Sierra Maestra* mountains in Oriente. I can tell by his tone that he has something serious to say. My father explains that Fidel and his victorious army are triumphantly marching through the country into Havana. I wonder if my neighbors will be joining Fidel, Raul, and *el Che*?

I don't know what to think. Will I have a job when I return to *La Habana*? Will it be safe to travel? Should I leave my aging parents and brothers and sisters during these tumultuous times? Will the promises of the Cuban Revolution come to fruition? It is too much to think about. I sit outside in the peaceful countryside smelling fresh grass and orange blossoms. I prop the radio on the windowsill. I cherish the music. I decide I will cherish the uncertainties. I cherish my life as a *Cubana*. I must follow the right path as it unfolds for me. I feel my life is in for some BIG changes.

CUBAN COUNTRYSIDE

Chapter 31

Be Strong, Havana

As soon as I am up, I hear the news.

Cubans smashing parking meters with baseball bats.

People trashing hotels and destroying casinos.

They are vandalizing stores and taking what they want.

"Fidel is on his way to Havana," my father says.

I know we will not be joining the thousands of Cubans marching with guns and machetes.

They are following their self-proclaimed leader, Fidel Castro, as he makes his way to the Capital.

"Be strong, Havana," I whisper.

I see all of our parents and my grandparents sitting at the long formal dining table.

Their faces are grim.

Everyone is talking at the same time.

Through all the voices, I hear my grandfather's words loud and clear: "Everyone is happy now, but later all will cry."

I try to listen to more of the discussion, but Papy sees me and shoos me away.

Children in Cuba are never privy to any serious information.

Mamy has tears in her eyes, "*Ay dios mio, ay dios mio.*"

I hear the anguish in her cries.

I go outside.

My street is quiet.

I hear distant explosions.

I see the Chinese man.

He is bringing our laundry.

I love to see him, especially when he has his children with him.

They remind me of my China dolls with their porcelain skin.

He is very efficient and marks each family's clothes with a special
black marking that distinguishes them, so they are not mixed
up when they arrive at CARDECUYOTU.

Yoly and Renecito come over to our house.

We go to the back yard.

We sit and talk about how cold it is.

I have Henry, my doll.

I named him from one of my favorite comics.

I enjoy reading about Henry, Archie, and other American characters.

Sometimes I cut up the paper comic strips from the *periodicos*.

I glue the cartoon characters onto cardboard and make my own
paper dolls.

I get the cardboard from the Chinese launderer.

He puts it in between each of my father's shirts so they stay
wrinkle-free.

Henry comes everywhere with me.

CUBY, YOLY, TENSY, & CARMEN

Chapter 32

The Hokey Pokey

After the revolution, Abuelo Delio was promptly ousted from his position on the Supreme Court of Cuba.

He had presided on the highest court of Cuba for years.

He served both the people of Cuba and his country for decades.

He met with former Presidents Ramón Grau, Carlos Prío-Socarrás, and Fulgencio Batisita.

Once President Grau came to CARDECUYOTU for dinner.

Neny and I were downstairs, and all the adults were sitting and chatting.

Neny, who was only about five, walked right over to Mamy, pointed to Grau, and said in a loud voice "Mamy, why is that man so ugly?"

Mamy was mortified.

Papy smiled.

Grau continued with his story, as if he was not fazed.

Abuelo's chauffer no longer comes to pick him up every day in his black limousine to take him to work.

He stays home now.

He reads.

He reads a lot.

It seemed now Fidel was the only one making laws and governing our country.

From what I could see, he wasn't doing a good job.

Things that we used every day were becoming a bit harder to get.

Suddenly, we feel a chill.
It gets even colder as Dulce, Tulito's nanny, appears out of nowhere.
She is old and white and is missing her front teeth.
Her gums are invisible.
Papy calls her a *comúnnanga*, a big communist.
No one in the family can talk freely against Fidel for fear she will
    be the informant to go to the neighborhood *comité* and snitch.
Dulce calls us *gusanos*, worms.
She leans down and says to us, "Enjoy it while you can. Someday
    you will lose it all — your house, your cars, even your dolls."
She is mean.
She is bitter.
She is crazy.
And she has bad breath.
What does she know?
CARDECUYOTU is OUR house.

I run inside and find my grandfather.
"Abuelo Delio, is it true that Fidel will take our house?"
He says, "Never, Cubitica. *No te preocupes*, don't worry. I will die
    in this house before anyone takes it from us."

Abuelo and I have mean games of canasta against Neny and Chuchin.
Abuelo and I are always partners.
These daily matches are taken very seriously by Abuelo — but not
    by Chuchin and Neny.
They laugh and they cheat.
It makes Abuelo very mad.

I can tell however that these games and the routine are helping him
deal with the difficult times that he is facing.

Abuela, who knows everything, calls us to the kitchen.
When she calls, we listen.
"I heard there will be a delivery of soap today," she begins.

We are still able to get most things we need, but there are a few
items that are in limited supply.
So when we get word of a shipment, we spread out like wolves.
We wait at different spots to be sure we will get what we need.

"Cuby and Reny, you go to *La Bonita*."
"Chuchin, you go to the other corner store."
"Tulito, you wait for the milk man at the corner. Get ours before
he runs out."
My brother and I head out.
We are ready for the quest.
We pass several houses with yellow papers stapled onto their
front doors.
"What are those?" I ask him.
"They are gone," he says. "Those families have left."
The houses belong to Fidel now.
I think about Dulce's warning, but I am not worried.
No one will ever take it.
Our house has our names on it.

Shortly after stealing our country, Fidel Castro began taking
businesses, closing many schools, and shutting down churches.
He was stripping us of all we had.

The new government was also sending the older boys to the Soviet Union to get their education, training them as soldiers, and indoctrinating them in the Communist way.

Fear hung heavy as the fog over the sugar cane fields.
We knew of many desperate families that had decided to send their children to America.
The children sometimes must go alone, since visas are difficult to get.
Families are racing the clock of communism that seemed to be ticking faster every day.
The long line starts before we even get close to *La Bonita*.
We find our spot and hear a catchy tune.
The mother behind us is singing it with her small son.
We hear them singing it over and over while we wait and, eventually, we hear the words coming off our lips ....

Primero de Mayo, Día del Trabajo.
Dame tu mano, trabajador.
Unidos todos, codo con codo.
Ya dirigimos nuestra nación!
No importa el sacrificio
Para el trabajador,
Mientras más nos agredan
Mas será nuestro ardor.

We are singing and smiling.
We get to the front of the line and race each other home.
Neny wins and enters the house singing our new song loudly.
"Nooooo!!! *Callate*!!!" Mamy screams. "Don't you EVER sing that again. They are brainwashing you."

I know the words of the songs are communist hoopla, but the
    chants and songs are very catchy.
I sing them all the time.
Sometimes I don't even realize I am singing them.
Mamy is fearful that they are winning us over.
I promise her to never sing that tune again.

"Who wants to play hokey pokey?" I say to change the subject.
Tonito raises his hand.
He is always ready for dancing.

I get my record player out, drop the needle and put my right-
    hand in.

CUBY DRIVEWAY

Primero de Mayo... Día del trabajo,
dame tu mano, trabajador.
Unidos todos, codo con codo,
ya dirigimos nuestra nación!
No importa el sacrificio
para el trabajador,
mientras más nos agredan
más será nuestro ardor.

Estudio... Trabajo... Fusil...
Nuestras armas en la lucha por la
paz.
Venceremos...Venceremos...Vencer
mos...
Unidad...Unidad...Unidad.
Primero de Mayo, Día del Trabajo,
Fiesta del mundo trabajador.
Unidos todos, codo con codo.
Será más fuerte nuestra razón!
La lucha nos enseña
la táctica mejor.
Unidos venceremos
a cualquier agresor.

Estudio... Trabajo... Fusil...
Nuestras armas en la lucha por la
paz.
Venceremos...Venceremos...
Venceremos...
Unidad...Unidad...Unidad.

Chapter 33

A World of Secrets

It is February 1961.
I wake up and go straight to Carmenchu's door and knock.
No answer.
I keep knocking.
No one is there.

"Where is Carmenchu?" I ask Mamy.
Carmenchu's whole family has flown to Jamaica together to escape.
They are the first to leave.
She was not allowed to say anything to us about going.
There are ears everywhere, even in our own house.
You never know who is listening.
Two fewer cousins to play with.

Mamy wants to escape and leave the island for a while.
Security is becoming tighter and tighter.

Communism was alive and well the first year.
But now you can tell who is a communist and who isn't.
No professionals were permitted to leave the island.
No doctors, no lawyers, no judges.
Visas are not freely given.
Parents are sending their children alone to America on airplanes
    to get them out of the country until the turmoil in Cuba ends.

Thousands of us are leaving Cuba without our parents, headed to
   the United States.
I wonder when it will be my time to go.

Things we have always had are becoming harder to get.
Lu never talks about it.
I have never seen her sad.
She is always smiling.
Her dimples like craters.
"Life is an adventure to be lived," she says.

I go downstairs and see the adults watching television.
They are watching something called *El Paredón*.
I see men being interviewed.
The next image on the screen shakes me.
I see several men lined up against a white wall.
They are the counter revolutionaries.
The militia takes out their rifles and shoot them down like
   dominoes.
I know I shouldn't watch, but it is hard to look away from the TV.
"No, *pequeña*," my grandfather says. "This is not for your eyes."
He has spotted me.
"This is not for your eyes," he repeats.
He makes me leave the room.
I pretend to go upstairs, but I sneak back and quietly watch.

I live in a world of secrets.

Chapter 34

The White Curb

It's Friday morning.

Pancho picks me up and we drive to school.

I see military men with guns at many street corners along the
way.

Things started to get even crazier after the Bay of Pigs fiasco in
April of 1961.

The bus drops me off, and I arrive at *Las Dominicas Americanas*,
my school.

Instead of the usual music and assembly in the courtyard, we are
led to the chapel.

We are greeted by men in uniforms.

Americans were the first to flee Cuba

All the American nuns at our school have left.

The American embassy is gone.

Our private schools have been taken over.

Papy warned that socialist and communist regimes have a knack
for indoctrinating the young.

They are feeding us students their communist propaganda.

Today, nuns are replaced with soldiers with guns and uniforms.

They make us sit down in the pews.

One by one, they take turns with bats to destroy and demolish all
the statues of Jesus, Mary, and Joseph.
They continue down the line until the chapel is filled with only
rubble and remnants of our holy saints.

Next we are ushered back to our classrooms.
Our teacher is gone.
A man in uniform says, "Sit and listen."
He then instructs is to take our pencils out.
I look to the front of the class.
The familiar gold crucifixes that had been hanging all year in
our classrooms are now replaced with huge framed portraits
of Lenin.
I am scared.
I can't wait to go home.

"You will not go back there," Mamy says as soon as she picks me
up for lunch.

It is Friday.
The fisherman comes to the door with his fresh catch — *pargo*.
Lu cooks the whole red snapper and brings it to the table.
Papy always makes it a big ceremony when he eats the eyeball.
Neny laughs and laughs.
I don't like to watch.
I fall asleep early and wake up even earlier.
I walk outside and see the Jeep.
"The Jeep is here! The Jeep is here!" I yell.
All the cousins scramble out of bed. They don't want to miss it.
We never know when it is coming, but as soon as I see it, I am
usually the first to follow.

143

There is a big white Jeep that comes around and fumigates for
    mosquitoes.
We run after it, unknowingly inhaling toxic fumes.

We get lost in the heavy cloud of pesticide.
The fun is instantaneous.
We don't even mind the strange smell.
Lu tells me it's OK to play behind the trucks. She even joins us!
She says it must not be real poison.
We still have mosquitoes everywhere.
And if it can't even kill a mosquito it shouldn't do any harm to us!
We are dancing and laughing in the clouds as we run behind it.

There is talk around the neighborhood that Yuri Gagarin, the first
    man in space, is coming to Havana.
The Russians have beat the Americans in the race to space.
The famous cosmonaut is coming to Havana as a hero, and Fidel
    wants to pay him homage.
The neighbors are painting the curb white, so it looks nice for his
    visit.
The communist *comité* in the neighborhood is sponsoring this
    event, giving out buckets of white paint to all who are willing
    to paint the curbs.
They ask Neny and I if we want to join them.
They are all enjoying themselves, so we grab a brush and start to
    paint.
The paint dries fast in the hot Cuban sun.
We make quick work of it since it is so much fun.
Mamy and Papy come out to the end of our driveway.
Papy grabs Neny's arm.
"Time to go," he says.

Once we are inside, our parents tell us we should not be getting our streets ready for the communists who are taking our country from us.

No one is free to speak their thoughts if they are against Fidel for fear of getting jailed or worse.

We keep quiet.

Only when there is the silence of the night, when servants, nannies, and neighbors are gone, do we speak of Castro's Cuba.

I pull the thin *mosquitero* back.

The netting helps protect me from the mosquitos while I sleep.

I think Lu is right.

The toxins from the Jeep must not be dangerous. Mosquitoes are everywhere.

The buzzing is even louder now.

Conga & Lu

NENY & CUBY

BROKEN STATUES

Chapter 35

Si Le Gusta, Se Repite

Sundays are fun family days.
Sundays are also Lu's day off.
She takes a bus to Matanzas to see her family.
I miss her when she is gone, but she always has great stories to tell
me Monday morning.

Today we go to Caway to ride horses in our cowboy suits.
I always want to be an Indian, but again today I am a cowgirl.
Our stomachs are rumbling; it's time to eat.
Papy drives to *Rancho Luna* for lunch.
It has the best barbecue!

Once our bellies are full, we drive downtown.
Papy says, "Who feels like a movie?"
We go to the *Cinema Astral*.
Papy buys the tickets.
Last time we were here, Mamy had to remind us to look for bombs
in the theater before we found our seats. The revolution is over,
but I look anyway.
All clear.

For one ticket we can watch two short cartoon flicks, a *noticiário*
or a newsreel, and the main attraction, which today was an
American movie, a Western called *The Magnificent Seven*.

Neny is in heaven.

He still has his cowboy suit on.

I know next time we play he will make me be the evil Calvera, and all the girls will be my band of outlaws.

The boys will ride horses and pretend they are the American Magnificent Seven and save the town.

We have become very fast readers, because most movies we see are in English with subtitles.

I am only able to read about half of the lines.

This movie is a bit boring to me.

My favorite movie star is Jerry Lewis.

I laugh out loud at all the funny faces he makes.

Papy and Neny try to imitate him, too.

It's so funny!

We are hungry again.

My stomach rumbles.

"Let's eat!" I say.

I see a mural painted on a building — it says "Viva Fidel."

At the next intersection, another wall's graffiti reads, "Fidel, the Cuban people are with you." Driving near the *Malecón*, I see an enormous painting of Che and Fidel, bearded and dressed in fatigues.

Signs of Fidel's victory are everywhere.

There are so many restaurants to choose from.

We usually pick one that serves exotic foods — Chinese, Arabian, or African.

I like *Qinbombo.*

Neny and I laugh when the waiter says, *"Si le gusta, se repite"* — if
  you like it, you can have seconds.

Today we vote on a drive-up joint.
I order a Cuban *frita* and a *batido*, a burger and shake.
Pure deliciousness.
There is nothing that compares to a Cuban *frita*.
It is a crispy, thin patty, toasted bun, and of course, chopped
  onions.
Mamy finishes her milkshake and orders another.
We give her strange looks and wonder where her tiny frame could
  keep anymore food.
"Si le gusta, se repite!" she says.

We laugh the whole way home.

Chapter 36

A Silent Kiss Goodbye

It is August 21, 1961.

Mamy and Papy call us into their room.

Papy's tone is serious. He says, "You will be leaving tomorrow for
Miami. You will be going with other children and no adults.
You will have many adventures, and then you will return to
us before long."

The Americans are working to help overthrow Castro.

"Do not worry," Papy tells us. "You will be home soon."

"Do not tell anyone," they say to us several times.

"Yes, we understand," we answer in unison.

"No one must know," they repeat.

I am not worried.

I feel exhilarated!

It is my turn to go!

I can't wait.

I have never flown on an airplane before!

The only "planes" I have ever ridden are the *guayaba* trees at
the *finca*.

It is August in Cuba.

The sun feels good on my skin.

I soak it in.

Conga & Lu

After roller-skating in the park, I follow Neny.
He is always a bit faster.
He goes back to the house, and instead of taking our skates off, we
    skate down the long hallway.
Tulito is throwing his baseball in the air.
We have to swerve to avoid him.

"Stop!" Lu says. "Your *abuela* doesn't like you skating in the house!"
We don't listen.
We glide smoothly over the shiny checkerboard floors, still wet in
    spots where they had been mopped them.

Mamy calls me upstairs.
She closes the door and says, "You can only bring one thing with
    you when you go to America tomorrow. What would you like
    to bring?"
I look around my room. I see Henry on my bed.
"I want to bring Henry with me," I say.
There was talk about more of us leaving, the second wave of Silvas,
    but even within our family things were very hush-hush.
Us kids are not told much.
That is the Cuban way.

They tell my brother and Chuchin they must bring a box of cigars.
They can sell them when they get to Miami for money.
Today Mamy will prepare our *croquetas*, the bags that will carry
    our clothes to Miami when it is our turn to go.

Last week we stopped at our seamstress, the same one who had
    always made our Mother's Day dresses. Now she will sew our
    bags.

Neny and I will have matching *croquetas*.

I choose an aqua and white striped pattern.

The sturdy duffel bag is made of canvas.

Then we went downtown.

We drove by soldiers on several corners, all armed with guns.

They are more present now than even a year ago.

Later, we went to *El Encanto*, the department store.

Mamy loves it there.

She bought me a blue blazer and a skirt.

Neny chose a brown suit.

Mamy told me to pick a new outfit for Henry, too.

I picked out a yellow polo, black shorts, and cute little booties.

He looked adorable.

I sit with Mamy, folding and rolling as many clothes as I can into
    my *croqueta*.

We are only permitted 50 pounds.

She knows they will search our bags.

I must leave all my wonderful toys, books, and games here in my
    room.

As we pack, I sneak my small rubber figurines of Orphan Annie,
    Dick Tracy, and the others in between my shirts.

No one will see them hidden inside my blouses.

Papy comes in and tells me tomorrow before I leave, he wants me
    to sneak a hundred-dollar bill in the back of my mouth.

He shows me where to conceal it, in the pocket of space close to
    my gums.

"No, Papy. That is disgusting. There is not enough room there, and
    money is dirty!"

He pleads with me, but I will not agree.

I will not sneak the money in my mouth.

Mamy has an idea.
She asks to see Henry.
She looks through my jewelry box.
I have many beautiful pieces.
She picks my gold chain out of the box.
"Cuby, you have this beautiful necklace. They will not let you wear
     it but let's put it on Henry. Then, if you need to, you can trade
     it for money in Florida."
I see the pain in her eyes.
I feel the sorrow in her voice but she manages to smile.
We slip it under his yellow polo, out of sight.

Later, we take a drive into Havana to have supper with my Abuela
     Iraida and Abuelo Pompeyo.
We visit with them every week.
My visits there are magical.
As we pull up, Papy reminds us, "You cannot say goodbye to Abuela.
     She must not know that you are leaving in the morning for the
     U.S.A. It is a secret that you must keep."
We nod.
I run upstairs to the second-floor apartment.
Linda, their dog, is of course the first to say hello.
While Abuela is cooking, I help Neny lower the bread basket so
     the vendors can fill it.
They also place vegetables and fruits inside.
It is heavy, but we raise it up and bring it to the kitchen.

Next, I go to the bedroom.

I smell the fragrant candles that are always burning in front of her
statue of San Lazaro.
Abuela Iraida had once told me it had been handed down from
generation to generation, as long as she could remember.
I can't wait until it comes to me.
My grandmother makes the most delicious chicken in all of Cuba.
She uses plenty of garlic and *mojo*.
I love to lick my fingers one by one when I am done to get every
last bit of flavor.
It may not be proper, but I can't help myself.

Linda sits near me the whole time.
I think she senses that I am leaving.
"See you next week!" Abuela Iraida says, as she squeezes me with
hugs.
Her plump body engulfs me, and her sweet smile seems to radiate
only for me.
My Abuela loves me.
We share a love of the simple things in life.
A love of stray animals and a love of music.
She is warm, happy, and real.
She reminds me of Lu in many ways.

I long to tell her I am taking a trip tomorrow, an adventure to
America, but Mamy and Papy have made me promise.
Linda gets one more sniff, and after a few more *besitos* and hugs
from my grandparents, we are gone.
Abuela Iraida doesn't know, but I say goodbye.

I send her a silent kiss goodbye.

ABUELA IRAIDA & LINDA

NEIGHBOR BRINGING UP BREAD

ABUELO POMPEYO & ABUELA IRAIDA'S APARTAMENT

Chapter 37

Leaving

I wish I could tell Lu I am leaving.
I must keep my promise and not say anything about my trip.
I don't question why.
I just eat my Cuban bread.
Mamy had gotten me an autograph book months ago.
Many adults and children get autograph books.

I have been asking everyone sign it.
I have autographs from my teachers, grandparents, friends, and
    cousins.
I had Mamy, Papy, Abuelo Delio, and Abuela sign.
I saved two pages for my Abuela Iraida and Abuelo Pompeyo.
They can sign when I return.
I get a pen and ask Lu to sign.
She writes,

Cuby,
I pray that happiness always smiles upon you and reigns in your
    heart.
Love, Lu

She is about to draw a picture for me, too, but Papy says it's time
    to go.
I whisper, "I love you, Lu."

I know my *croquetas* are packed and waiting for me in the car.
I get up.
I look back to see Lu clearing the table.
I wave to her and send a kiss.
Another silent kiss goodbye.

I will miss my Lu, but I know she will be so excited for me once she
knows I am going to Miami.
I wish I could ask her what she wants me to bring her back from
the U.S.A.

"Your Aunt Chucha will meet you at the airport in Miami," Mamy
says, as we drive to the airport.
Carmenchu's father Cuco was able to fly his family from Jamaica
to Florida.
He has a job for a small Spanish business as a janitor, teacher,
chauffer, and accountant.
Anything that needed to be done, he is the man to do it.
Cuco was able to rent a small apartment in Miami.
"You will stay with them until it is safe for you to come back home."

I can see the signs for Rancho Boyeros Airport.

Our journey begins!

CUBY'S AUTOGRAPHS

159

Chapter 38

La Pescera

We arrive at Rancho Boyeros Airport.

Mamy struggles to walk.

She grasps my tiny hand tightly in one of hers and Neny's in her other.

Her legs almost give out.

We are helping to keep her up.

Her tears flow, leaving a river behind her as her high heels click the cement.

Papy carries my giant *croqueta* to the doors.

At eleven, Neny is a man now.

He will carry his own bag.

Papy tells him he must take care of me in Miami.

Our cousin Chuchin will be going with us, too.

He is 15 years old.

We are all very nervous for him.

Families live in fear that their boys will be taken to the Soviet Union, given guns, indoctrinated, and trained as communist soldiers.

Papy, who was the most influential of the family as a judge, was the first to be able to get three visas to the U.S. through the Spanish Embassy.

Abuela knew that Chuchin must get out of Cuba before he is sent to the Soviet Union or wherever the Communist regime would send young soldiers to be trained or to fight.

I see so many families being torn apart.
I hear crying.
White handkerchiefs are wiping noses and drying eyes.
They look like white clouds against the backdrop of the beautiful
    blue Havana sky.
I am surrounded by sorrow and heartache.

But my feelings are different.
I am feeling excited.
I am going to America!
I will get to see what my older cousins and my parents have been
    able to see.
Abuela normally takes each of her grandchildren to America when
    they turn 15.
Mamy and Papy had their honeymoon there, too.
They saw everything from Miami to Niagara Falls.

The land of Barbies and Raggedy Ann dolls.
I will wear stretch pants and turtlenecks.
I will eat Burger King cheeseburgers, Pixy Stix, and Ruffles potato
    chips!
I will chew gum again!
Chiclets and Bazooka, oh have I missed you!
Since the U.S.A. has blocked items from entering Cuba, I have not
    been able to buy my favorite candies.
I may even meet Elvis Presley and Jerry Lewis.
I will do the Twist with Chubby Checker!
America the beautiful!
I will soon be there!

Conga & Lu

My mind wanders.
I am already at the front of the long line of children about to enter
   the *pescera*, the glass dome that looks like a fishbowl.
We are showered with kisses and hugged so hard it takes our
   breath away.
We show our papers and are shuffled through a doorway and into
   la *pescera*, the fishbowl.

Once we are put inside the fishbowl we cannot get out.
I wait and wait and wait.
I watch the parents' sorrows on the outside of the bowl and hear
   sobs of children all around me on the inside.
Neny is sure to keep my hand in his.
He doesn't let go.
We catch glimpses of Mamy in her floral dress, still crying.
She is beautiful.
My father stands steady and waves when he catches my eye.

It is crowded, hot, and smelly in the bowl.
They give us some peanuts and we wait.
After we wait, we wait some more.
Finally, the door of the fishbowl opens.

America, here I come.

CUBY PASSPORT

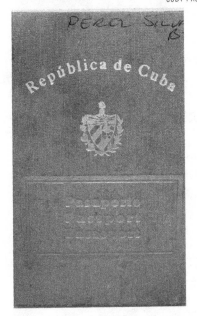

AUGUST 22, 1961

163

Chapter 39

Little Blue Lights

It's our turn.
It is dusk now.
We walk onto the tarmac.
We board the Pan Am flight bound for Miami.
I sit in the seat next to the window.
Neny is next to me, and Chuchin is by the aisle.
The excitement is building.
A blonde stewardess helps me buckle my seat belt.

Neny looks past my shoulders and out the window.
He is looking for Mamy.
There are many people standing outside, but they are far from
    the plane.
"I see her!" he says.
"I can't tell who she is," I say.
"There, over there! Her hands are blocking her face," he tells me.
She must be wiping away her tears

I look over at Neny.
Tears well up in his eyes.
It seems that the crying on the plane is contagious.
It is loud.
It is sad.
But I am ready.

Henry is ready.
No one else around us is ready.

Finally, our plane is moving faster and faster.
We run like Tormenta, then ...
We are flying!
I see my beautiful Havana — the tall buildings, palm trees, greens
    of every shade, crystal-blue water, all getting farther and farther
    away.
We are in the clouds.
All is white.
Adios!

Our flight is short, but the constant cries make it seem like an eternity.
I hear every kind of cry imaginable.
Whimpers, weeping, wailing, whining, bawling, and gut-
    wrenching screams.
There are red eyes and sniffles all around me.
There are enough tears shed to fill the pool at *El Comodoro.*
But not me.
I am confident.
I always have been.

There are only children on board.
I see two-year-olds, grade-schoolers, and teenagers.
I am not sad.
This is a grand adventure.
I can fly, I can fly, I can fly!

In Cuba, the first day of kindergarten is a traumatic affair, with
    kids bawling and clinging to their parents.

Conga & Lu

I remember Neny started school before me.
Papy had to sit for weeks in the last row of the classroom.
Neny kept looking back saying, "*Papy, no te vayas*" — don't go,
  Papy.
Two years later was my turn.
Mamy was hoping I would be a crying fool clinging to her, but
  instead, amidst all the other foolish girls crying with nuns
  trying to pry them away from their mothers, there I was just
  standing contently next to Mamy outside the classroom door.
After a while, I said to her, "Well, *vete*! Go!"
So she left, and I skipped into the room all by myself, as Mamy left
  a crying mess.

I keep adjusting myself to get comfortable.
My skinny legs don't quite touch the floor.
Neny is talking to Chuchin.
I peer out the window, and I see them.
They are easy to see on the landing strip in the dark sky.
Little blue lights guiding us to freedom.
We have arrived.
Los Estados Unidos.
The UNITED STATES OF AMERICA!

I am small, but I am great.
Not only am I great, I am the best.
But, isn't everyone?

Let's go.

CUBY'S FAVORITE RUBBER FIGURINES THAT TRAVELED FROM CUBA

Chapter 40

Days of Waiting

It is the morning of the 22nd of August. I enter the kitchen and find Neny taking the last bite of his *pan*.

"Lu, remember my old autograph book?" says Conga. "Will you sign it for me and draw me one of your pretty pictures?" The book is pale blue. I see the special page she has saved for me. I write a quick message to her.

As I am thinking of what to draw, Señor René says, *"No hay tiempo."* There's no time. I pick up the breakfast dishes and clear the table. Conga gets into the car with her Mamy, Papy, Neny, and Chuchin. She yells, "See you later, Lu!" Señora Cubita tells me not to make lunch and dinner today.

I wish Fela were still next door. I miss her. After Carmenchu's family left Havana, she went back to her home in Oriente. Today seems very long. I clean the house and do the necessary chores. There is an uneasiness within me. As darkness approaches and still no sign of Conga or the family, I turn the radio on. Music heals and distracts me. I take a walk in the park. Rosa and a few others are out. We walk and talk. I am not in the mood for *chistes* (jokes) and small talk. My mind is someplace else.

I strain my eyes and see in the distance their Hudson coming down Figueroa Street. I run down the steps of *Parque Mendoza*. I am out of breath. I find Señor René and Señora Cubita walking hand in hand slowly with their heads bent towards the ground. There is no sign of Conga, no sign of Neny, and no sign of Chuchin. I know they are gone. My stomach feels queasy.

The next morning Señor René calls me over. "Negrita," he says, "Cuby and Reny have left. They have gone to the United States. They will be back soon when the troubles in Cuba disappear. Ears listen everywhere. The communist neighborhood *comité* cannot find out. Cubita and I will continue with our daily lives. No one will know they have left."

I break down and cry. Our goodbyes remain unsaid. I must stay strong. Señor René and Señora Cubita need me. They are trying to keep up appearances, but they do not look the same. Nothing is the same. The little girl who I adore is gone. I will wait for her.

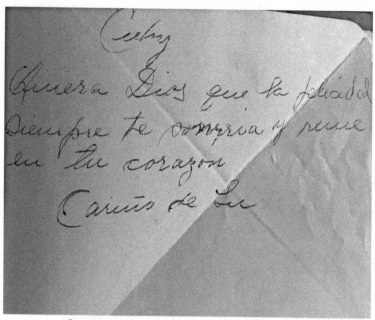

Cielin

Quiera Dios que la felicidad
siempre te sonría y reine
en tu corazón
Cariños de Lu

SEÑORA CUBITA

SEÑOR RENÉ

Chapter 41

Miami

We get off the plane.
It is hot and muggy.
The air feels heavy.
I look around and see so many other airplanes.
We walk down a corridor and enter the airport.
All of us are taken to a big room.
A nice lady brings us some water and some gum!
I unwrap it and immediately begin to chew.
Oh, have I missed gum!

They look at our passports and visas.
We sit and wait.
Papers are shuffled, folders created, phones ring.
We talk to some of the other children who are waiting.
They do not have family here.
They will be sent to group homes — orphanages set up for Cuban
    refugee children.
They will be going to camps in Matacumbe, Florida City, and Kendall.
I hear they are even separating siblings.
I feel so lucky. We don't have to go there.
We have some relatives already here in Miami.
I hug Henry tighter.
I am glad my cousin Chuchin is with us.
He is answering all the questions.

I do not know the answers.
A little bit of fear starts to visit me.

After several long hours, we are downstairs.
We are greeted with hugs and kisses by Aunt Chucha, Carmenchu,
    Uncle Cuco, and Cuquito.
Chucha cries.
I am so excited to see my cousin Carmenchu.

We get to the house.
It is not at all like CARDECUYOTU.
It is not majestic or grand.
It is small and shaped like a box.
I walk inside.
There are seven of us.
Our home has two bedrooms, one bathroom, a kitchen, and a
    living room.
I will stay in Carmenchu's room.
We stay up and talk all night long.
We are too excited to sleep.
After sleeping in all morning, we go back to the airport.
Cousin Tulito has arrived from Cuba, just a day after us!
He brings me love from Mamy and Papy and Lu.
Now there are eight in our new home.

Weeks later, my Abuela Cuba is the next to arrive.
Cousin Tensy is with her.

Abuela left her husband, her home, her friends, and her family.
She left her homeland to take care of us all while we are here in
    Miami, waiting for Cuba to be free of Fidel.

Abuela decided she needed to be here to support us.

Her Cuba had changed, and at least for the time being, it is not safe.

As her parents had done during the Spanish-American War, Abuela sought refuge in the open arms of America once again.

And just like that, our house added two more occupants.

MIAMI

CUBY, CUQUITO
RENY, TENSY, CARMENCHU, CHUCHA, ABUELA, CHUCHIN

Chapter 42

Milky Ways

It's Saturday.

We take the bus to the Cuban Refugee Center.

El Refugio is our one-stop "shopping."

The center is great.

The food is abundant, and the price is right, although they do not have much of a variety.

We are given a block of cheese in a brown box, powdered milk, powdered eggs, Spam, and all kinds of food we have never heard of or tasted.

One new food is called peanut butter.

I dip my finger in the jar as soon as we get it.

"*Que asco*, how horrible!" I say.

Everyone else tries it.

We agree what a disgusting food it is and wonder how people eat it.

I sure miss Lu's plantains and *picadillo*.

I close my eyes and can almost taste it.

"*Vamos*, let's go," Abuela commands.

Next we get to "buy" clothes.

Clean clothes are plentiful, and we feel good in our new outfits.

Today Cuquito and his whole family get *Mandrake el Mago* coats, Neny a pointed-tail shirt, and I get saddle shoes.

Boy, do we look sharp.

Unfortunately, a trip to *El Refugio* is not complete without getting
    our shots.
The vaccinations are also plentiful here.
Today I get a check-up and a vaccine.
Somehow when Abuela gave us our shots in Cuba they hurt a lot
    less.
I also do not like where they put the thermometers in America.
They go in and out of strange places, not the usual place under my
    arm like I was accustomed to in Cuba.

Looking good and feeling better now that the shots are over, we
    return home.
A letter is here!
It is for me!
Papy and Mamy send letters telling us they will see us soon.
I wonder if we will see them back in Cuba, or if they will get to
    come to Miami for a bit, too.

Enclosed is a dollar from Papy.
He instructs me to go to the Rexall on the corner and buy a Milky
    Way for a nickel.
Those are his favorite.
I think they are mine, too.

I buy a Milky Way and a pack of Juicy Fruit gum.
I write back to my parents and let them know all is well.
I put a few sticks of gum in the envelope.
One for Lu, and the others for my cousins Renecito, Yoly, and
    Tonito.

I seal it with a kiss.

Chapter 43

Shenandoah Elementary

It is my first day of school in America.

I walk a short distance to Shenandoah Elementary.

I get to my class and am surprised to see so many Cuban boys and girls.

I am also not used to seeing boys at school.

My teacher, Mr. Cunningham, introduces himself.

Mr. Cunningham is a long, lanky man.

He seems a bit odd and is wearing blue suspenders.

He seems unsure about what to do.

He does not speak Spanish, and for some of us, our English does not go beyond "Appy BirDAY tu u."

He takes out a ukulele and begins singing.

The Americans all join in.

"This land is your land, this land is my land."

He pauses, we all stare at each other, then he begins to sing again.

"Oh, my darlin', oh my darlin', oh my darlin' Clementine."

We start to join in and laugh and smile.

"One more," he says.

He sings,

"She'll be coming round the mountain when she comes (toot, toot).
She'll be coming round the mountain when she comes (toot, toot).
She'll be coming round the mountain, she'll be coming round
  the mountain,
She'll be coming round the mountain when she comes (toot, toot)."

By the end, we all add the sound effects and are laughing.
We are learning English with these songs and his strange-looking
  ukulele.

A bell rings.
It's time for lunch.
I am hungry.
I hope the food is better than our Spam sandwiches.

Today is spaghetti, peaches, green beans, and bread!
I even drink the milk.
Milk from cartons tastes better, I think.

After lunch, we get to play.
Our hokey pokey is replaced by "swing your partner *dos y dos.*"
The boys go to the field.
Some Americans are playing football.
Tulito looks puzzled.
We have not played with that odd-shaped ball before.
He doesn't seem too good at it.
He will have to practice.

There are so many Cubans here!
I easily bond with several girls in my grade.

Many of us have left our Cuban lives of luxury and have much
in common.
We talk of Havana and of our new experiences here in Miami.

We go back inside.
It is time for math.
Long division looks different than the way I was learning in Cuba,
but my knowledge of the subject matter is great.
Mr. Cunningham seems very impressed.
I think he is trying to tell me that I could move up a grade level, but
I don't quite understand what he is trying to say.
Most Cuban students that come seem to be working at a higher
level than those from the Miami public school.
Some of us are placed into a higher grade.
School is fun.
I can't wait to go back.
I sing the whole way home.

"This land was made for you and me."

CUBY AT SHENANDOAH

Chapter 44

Sports

I learn that Cubans are athletic.

We do a lot of sports in our new school.

I don't know how and why, but the Cuban teams always beat the
Americans by far in everything.

Everything except for football, which the poor Cubanitos had
never played before.

I am the star softball player, alternating key positions of pitcher
and first baseman with my friend, Olga Nazario.

I win all track running events and come home with many ribbons.

In volleyball, I'm short, but it doesn't matter. I am fast and agile,
flying around the court.

The Cuban sun has made us strong and fierce.

Our sense of competition is always kicked into high gear.

I guess the daily and nightly games of kickball and baseball at the
park across the street have paid off.

I wish my school had a pool like Neny's does, so I could blow every
opponent out of the water.

I truly believe in myself.

I feel all human beings must believe, they too are the best.

If you don't think you are exceptional, then who will?

It doesn't mean that I consider myself better than the rest, just that I am great, and everyone else probably thinks that they are great, too.

We follow the space race from the other shore now.
We watch as the Iron Curtain becomes heavier.
We are glad we are on northern shores, but not a minute of our existence do we ever think this exile is permanent.
We know it is temporary.
We are refugees who are only here for a brief stay in exile.
We will soon be returning to Cuba, our home.
We will see the gumbo limbo trees peeling in the sun.
We will feel the warm breeze as we watch the boats drift by from the *Malecón*.
We will hear the crickets chirping in the morning hours.
We will taste the fresh lechon that Frijolito prepares for us.
We will swim out to the *balsa*, racing the colorful parrot fish.

We all learn to support and help each other.
Under Abuela's care, we have become stronger, sounder, and more self-reliant.
She is our commander-in-chief.
We shop together, eat together, play together, and sleep together.
We experience the sorrows of separation and the joys of reunions.

With togetherness, we are complete.

MIAMI INTERNATIONAL AIRPORT – MORE SILVAS ARRIVE

CUBY'S RIBBON

Chapter 45

Free Turkeys

In Miami, we don't have the amenities and luxury items that we
  had in Cuba, but I do not miss them.
No TV, no radio, and no toys, but our time inside is minimal.
We are always outside.

We have grown used to Spam.
We no longer need to ask Abuela what's for dinner.
We know the answer will have Spam in it.
Spam and eggs for breakfast, Spam sandwiches for lunch.
Dinner choices were Spam *croquetas*, Spam stew, Spam rice, and
  even Spam spaghetti.
Abuela became our "Spamish Queen."
The adults never needed to go on diets.
They all soon lost weight.

Everyone at school is talking about a holiday called Halloween.
We have never experienced it.
The Americans tell us we can dress up in costumes, knock on
  doors, say, "Trick or treat," and get free candy.
It sounds like a dream come true.
I was always scared but intrigued by the masks and costumes
  during the annual *Carnaval* in Havana.
I had nightmares for days.

I wonder if Halloween will be scary, too?

I miss celebrating holidays.
My last year in Cuba we did not get to celebrate much.
20 de Mayo — Cuba's Independence Day, which had become our
     family's biggest celebration — was no longer celebrated.
Castro had replaced it with July 26th, the beginning of his Cuban
     revolution.
Our Catholic churches were closed and banned, so we had no
     Christmas and no Easter.
Fidel took those away from us, too.
He replaced them with *Primero de Mayo* (workers' day) and other
     strange ones that were not fun at all.
Halloween is everything I thought it would be.
We get so much candy we ration it.
We eat Pixy Stix and Milky Ways all through November.

Soon they say it will be Thanksgiving, another holiday that is
     foreign to us.
Americans give thanks and celebrate the friendship feast that the
     Pilgrims of Plymouth and the Indians had together.
People watch football and eat turkey.
It is Wednesday, the day before Thanksgiving.
We hear our names on the loudspeaker, "Cuba Pérez-Silva, Tulio
     Silva, please report to the principal's office."
All the other students gasp.
They think we must be in trouble.
I am happy.
It is fun to hear my name called.

I walk to the office with my shoulders back and my head held high.

The principal tells me to wait there.

Tulito joins me.

Our principal returns moments later with a giant frozen turkey.

We can't believe our luck.

He tells us a few turkeys were donated for needy families, and we
had been chosen to receive one.

"Wow! How lucky are we!" we tell each other.

We proudly bring home the turkey, our trophy, taking turns
carrying the immensely heavy bird. We put it on our heads
for all to see.

Others point at us.

"They must be jealous! What comemierdas!" we say.

The turkey is so tremendously big that I can barely carry it.

It is sweating in the Florida heat.

But it keeps me cool.

It feels like it is almost thawed out and ready to cook.

We can't wait to get home and show Abuela our tasty treat.

Abuela is overjoyed.

That turkey gets marinated and goes into the oven that night.

It is Thanksgiving.

We have a turkey.

We sit at the table, on the couch, wherever there is room to eat.

We say grace.

It is my turn.

"Thank you, God, for this delicious meal. Thank you for my
family, my friends, and Miami."

We each say what we are thankful for.

We say a prayer for everyone in Cuba.

I say an extra prayer for Mamy, Papy, Lu, Abuelo, and all the
animals at *la finca*.
There is much to be thankful for.

No Spam tonight!

CUBY, FAMILY, & FRIENDS AT CARNAVAL IN CUBA — MISSING OUR CUBAN HOLIDAYS

EL REFUGIO

Chapter 46

The Best Present

Our house has an open-door policy.
Guests come for a weekend and stay for a month.
I learn a lot sharing a home with so many different personalities
in such a small space.
We all must learn to adjust and modify.
In each of the bedrooms, we have a double bed plus bunk beds.
Aunt Chucha and Uncle Cuco share a room, with Neny and
Cuquito on the bunk beds.
Tensy and Abuela share a bed in the other room, with me and
Carmenchu on the bunk beds. Chuchin sleeps on the couch
and Tulito's special bed is made of two chairs in the dining
room. We joke that his blanket is the phone.
His nightly prayer, "No phone calls tonight, please God."
There are ten of us in the two-bedroom home.
And our porch is always filled with friends.

It has been four months since I have seen Mamy and Papy.
I miss them greatly.
I am having a lot of fun in Miami, but I wish they could join
us here.
Oh, the laughs we would have ....
I also miss Lu.
I miss telling her about my day and hearing about hers.
I miss the way we would talk.

I could ask her anything, and she always had a way to put things
     so that I understood them.
Sometimes she wouldn't even need to speak.
We knew what the other was thinking.
I hope she is keeping busy with Neny and I gone.
She loves when I send gum.
I will send more soon.

Christmas is coming, and Chucha takes us to *El Refugio.*
She goes into a room and comes out with some bags.
"No peeking," she proclaims.
She has just gotten our Christmas presents.
I can't wait for mine.
We are headed back to the airport.
Who will it be today!

As I sit waiting, I stare at the tile floor in the airport.
I follow the grout lines with my eyes creating a maze.
There is something familiar about the black high heels coming in
     my direction.
I recognize those *tacones* clicking in the distance.
As my eyes scan upward, I notice the dress she was wearing the
     day we left.
My eyes move even higher.
Am I dreaming?
Mamy? Papy?
They have arrived!

The government had taken everything — our home, our cars, our
     money, our freedom — everything.
But none of that mattered.

We are united again.
The four of us embrace for an eternity.
All is right in the world.
This is the best Christmas present I have ever received.
I don't even care what Santa is bringing.

At the house, we sit around the table and listen to Papy's story of how he was able to flee the country by the skin of his teeth.

"As I left work at the bureau, I turned to all the girls still working at their desks. 'Adios, muchachitas. See you tomorrow!' I told them as I tried to act as if everything were normal. We went to the airport early this morning. Your mother and I were only able to take one bag each. Security is even tighter than it was when we sent you *hijos*. No one comes in or goes out without military approval and proper documentation. Mamy was sad to leave our belongings, photos, jewelry, everything. It was difficult for her to leave home, your Abuelo Delio, and your Aunt Yolanda. We had the opportunity to go, so we had to take it. It was very painful living without you both. We love Cuba, but what is happening there is a terrible tragedy. At the airport, Castro's military is everywhere. Soldiers with guns are checking papers of all Cubans wanting to leave. There are long lines of people. We must have waited for hours. We witnessed crying and families embracing. People's faces look defeated and sad. We finally got to the gate, and the man scrutinized our papers. 'Dr. René Pérez-Amargos,' he says, 'Confirm your occupation.' 'I am a judge,' I say. He whistles, and right away another guard appears. Your Mamy is a basket case by now. She can barely stand. 'You know diplomats and judges are not permitted to leave the island,' the soldier says.

'Show me the papers saying you have resigned. You must come with us,' they say. I stayed confident and quickly collected my thoughts. I must act quickly. With a forceful voice, I said, 'DO YOU NOT UNDERSTAND THAT A JUDGE DOES NOT HAVE TO SIGN PAPERS TO RESIGN? A JUDGE RESIGNS VERBALLY BEFORE HIS COURT, AS I HAVE DONE, AND I AM FREE TO GO!' The men look bewildered as they talk to each other trying to figure out what to do. I bluffed again, 'Would you like me to call the court right now? I highly doubt they would like to be bothered with such a trivial matter during their already busy day. They may have your job for it.' 'Let them go,' one guard says to the other. They stamped our passports and escorted us to the plane. Once we were seated and in the air, I said to Mamy, 'That was close.' I was terrified. We were one step from jail."

"You are a hero," Mamy says. "I love you."
It is great to be together.
Papy is the first one in line at confession that week.

Sometimes a lie is necessary.

MAMY & PAPY

Chapter 47

More Goodbyes

Señora Cubita and Señor René have gone. I knew it was only a matter of time before they would join Cuby and Reny. I am very sad they are no longer here but overjoyed they will be with their children once again. Señor Delio is the only one remaining at the house now. Although I no longer work as a domestic, he tells me the apartment is mine and I will always be taken care of by him. I spend my days helping him in every way I can. He welcomes me into CARDECUYOTU, and we eat meals together at the enormous table. He sits and rocks most of the day. I know his mind is on his family often. The only daughter of his that remains in Cuba is Señora Yolanda. She lives in Altahabana, a new modern neighborhood. She visits daily. I wonder when all the family will be able to return. I miss the way things were. I also miss Conga deeply. I miss the family. Loneliness is creeping into my soul.

Conga & Lu

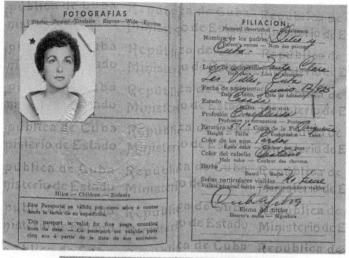

MAMY & PAPY'S PASSPORTS

Chapter 48

Suela, Zapato y Tacon

While we are learning English, so are our parents.
The adults in Miami all go together at night to Miami Senior High
   School to learn, or "improve" their English, except for Abuela.
She stays home and takes care of all things at the house.
They all come home singing, "I've been working on the railroad."
Their English has not improved much, but at least they have
   learned a new song.
Like us, our parents have a drive to learn and assimilate into the
   American culture, always.

Money is now scarce.
All the boys get jobs.
Before the sun rises, Renecito and Chuchin are up before anyone.
They take a bus to pick strawberries.
A few hours later, they come home, earlier than usual.
"Why are you home so soon?" I ask.
"We got fired," they say together.
Renecito laughs, "Those strawberries were so tempting and
   delicious! They told us that we eat more than we pick. They
   removed us from the fields and didn't even want us to finish
   our shift."
He smiles and empties his pockets overflowing with strawberries.
They are smooshed, but we don't care.
We each grab a juicy berry.

They enter the circle, and we continue the game.

It is called *Suela, Zapato y Tacon.*

We're not sure who made this game up or where it came from.

We play this game of categories for hours.

To play, we clap and snap to a beat.

You must say something from the chosen category, on the beat, or you are out.

Neny and Renecito are the last ones in.

Girls have already lost.

Now they continue to see who is king.

Names of ... brands of ... motorcycles: BMW snap snap, Harley-Davidson snap snap, Moto Guzzi snap snap, Triumph snap snap.

Neny pauses for too long.

"Honda," he says, but it is not in time.

Boys win again.

We spend hours taxing our memories coming up with names of cars, cereals, detergents, countries, and any category we could think of.

The local A&P on *Calle Ocho* in Miami served as our fountain of knowledge.

We would walk the endless aisles for hours memorizing cookie boxes, soaps, shampoos, everything.

It was so different than *La Bonita* in Cuba.

All sorts of food all together in one place — meat, bread, fruits, anything you can think of!

They even have giant toys on the top of the aisles!

"Where is Tulito?" Neny says in between rounds.

No one knows.

"I last saw him in the A&P," Tensy says.

The phone rings.

Abuela hurries out.

She is gone no more than fifteen minutes but returns with Tulito.

The security guard at the A&P had followed him up and down the aisles.

The more he followed him, the more Tulito ran.

The officer could not comprehend why this boy was staring for so long at boxes of ice cream.

Tulito calmly sits down next to me.

He chooses the category.

"Names of ... brands of ... ICE CREAM."

He easily wins the round.

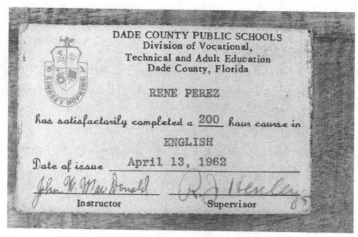

DADE COUNTY PUBLIC SCHOOLS
Division of Vocational,
Technical and Adult Education
Dade County, Florida

RENE PEREZ

has satisfactorily completed a 200 hour course in

ENGLISH

Date of issue   April 13, 1962

Instructor   Supervisor

PAPY'S ENGLISH COURSE PASSED

Chapter 49

El Camello

It is easy to get around Miami.

We walk, we take buses, we drive, and we bike.

Papy saved ten dollars and bought me a used bicycle from the mechanic.

We painted it blue and it looks as good as new to me.

While he was there, the mechanic also talked Papy into buying a car for 100 dollars.

My bike is wonderful.

I ride around the neighborhood, but almost never by myself.

We take it to school and back, four of us on it.

I stand up and pedal, Tulito rides on the front grill, and my friend Olga on the back.

We usually pick someone up along the way.

They always get to ride on the seat.

I love my bike.

We all enjoy riding in Papy's car, too.

We call it *El Camello*, the camel.

Our family outings never stop.

Today we are headed to the beach!

It is a tight squeeze with all twelve of us packed tight and piled high in *El Camello*.

The beach is a very short distance from our house, but we have
  already stopped several times for *El Camello.*
"Again?" we complain.
Papy pulls off to the side of the road and pulls out one of the gallons
  of water from the trunk.
"The Camel is thirsty" he says. "He needs to drink a lot of water."
We must go through at least three gallons before we reach the beach.
"What do you expect for 100 dollars?" Papy says.

We dive into the water, which is refreshing but not as clear as Cuba's.
I miss the fish who used to swim near my toes.
I smell Coppertone on the many bodies that cover the sand.

After the beach, we decide to go to the movies.
I have not seen a movie since Cuba!
We are all so very excited.
Our English has greatly improved, and we will be able to
  understand so much more!
We decide on Chubby Checker's "Twist Around the Clock."

Tulito runs into the front of the theater blocking the screen from
  the audience.
He starts copying Chubby's dance moves and begins to do the twist.
He is a dancing fool.
Two ushers walk up, each grabbing one of his arms.
As they lift him, his feet are still moving, and he dances his way
  down the aisle.
They finally remove him from the theater.
We almost pee our pants from laughing so hard.

He has become our family's own overnight sensation!

EL CAMELLO

MIAMI
BEACH

Chapter 50

Concerts

It is Saturday afternoon. I sit on the front porch and write a quick note to Conga on the back of a photo I will send her. The weather is dreamy. They are setting up for the concert in the park, where the government hosts free concerts. I attend them all. I love music. I bring a blanket and find a spot on the lawn.

I am near the memorial they erected for the revolutionary who killed himself while placing a bomb in the park. I remember the day it happened. Conga and Reny were very frightened. They came running upstairs to tell me about it. Seeing the bloodied man on their porch struggling to survive is something they will never forget. They play classical pieces, and Stravinsky, a Russian composer, is featured today. My favorites are the violins. The music fills the air, and even the birds seem to know when to sing. It is a beautiful concert.

Once it is over, Rita and I talk about going to the movies. I am not sure what is playing. Most movies are in Russian or in the Czech language. They are even harder to follow than the American movies we used to watch. We decide to skip the movies. She comes over and we sit and play cards for hours.

"AN OFFERING TO LIBERTY
FRANCISCO CARDONA ORTA
1930-1957
TO THE MEMORY OF THE BRAVE COMRADE WHO WAS SACRIFICED
DURING THE RUTHLESS TYRANNY.
DEATH DOES NOT OCCUR WHEN THE ACT HAS BEEN EXECUTED WELL."

MAIL FROM LU

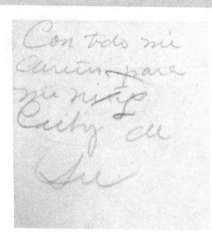

"With all my
love for
my girl
Cuby
from Lu"

Chapter 51

Chicken Pox

Turkey soup.

I can smell it cooking from the front yard.

Abuela had finally managed to cook every single piece of that turkey.

I think we even ate the bones last week.

Staring at me in the mirror is one big red pimple.

Cuquito laughs at it.

He says I must be starting "puberty."

I'm not exactly sure what that word means, but I'm fine without it.

I'll find out at my *quinceañera*, I guess.

Who wants pimples?

I decide to go outside and take my bike for a ride with my friends.

I return after a short time.

I'm unusually hot and sweaty.

I take a break, and Abuela brings me some water.

"*Ay Dios mio*, Cubitica," she exclaims.

"You have the chicken pox."

In a matter of hours, my pimple had multiplied from one to one hundred.

And unfortunately, within a matter of days, everyone in the house
was covered in the itchy spots.
All thirteen of us scratching and complaining.
But laughing all the while, because we were all in it together.

At least we have turkey soup to help us recover.

CUBY AND HER BIKE

Chapter 52

Conga Line

Miami International Airport sees our tears for those leaving for the North and our joys for those arriving from Havana.
Almost everyone in my family has left Cuba.
Tonito and his parents have left the island and are in Spain.
Aunt Yolanda and Uncle René I am sure will be here soon.

I miss Abuelo Delio, who has promised to look after our house until it is safe for us to come back home.
I miss our daily canasta games.
I miss Abuela Iraida, too.
I hope she knows I am well and will help her bring up the bread basket soon.
I also miss Lu terribly.
I hope she is taking my place at the table and playing canasta with Abuelo.
They are both very fine players.
I wonder who wins?

The usual number of people living in our house in Miami at one time is a dozen or maybe thirteen.
Problem-solving is our way of life.
We hear a knock on the door.
I peep out the window and see the landlord.
We have practiced the drill.

Some of us hide under beds or in closets and some run out the
  back door.
We try to hide the exorbitant number of blankets, cots, and
  pillows.

Luckily for us, Chucho's shirt is hanging outside.
Chucho has a job at the fishery, scaling fish.
The smell of snapper absorbs into his clothes.
Our landlord chooses not to enter.
He can't take the smell.

After the close call, Papy decides we must look for a bigger home.
He drives around in the Camel searching for a place, but many say
  no kids allowed.
He is having horrible luck.

We decide to write our Hymn of the Family.
We sing it to the tune of *El Himno Invasor*:

Adelante de nuevo familia,
Porque el dueño nos quiere botar.
El viejito chivato de al lado
Nos impulsa de nuevo a buscar.

Al Norwes, al Souwes, a Hialeah,
Donde iremos nosotros a parar?
Porque en Miami no quieren muchachos,
Porque vienen todos a chivar.

Buscamos el Miami Herald,
Encontramos a "House for Rent."

Pero al decir somos una docena,
Nos responden, "Go to the Hell."

Forward again family,
Because the owner wants to throw us out.
The old snitch next-door neighbor
Drives us back to looking again.

To the Northwest, to the Southwest, to Hialeah,
Where will we stop?
Because in Miami they don't want kids,
Because they come to annoy.

We look in the Miami Herald,
We find a "House for Rent."
But when we say we are a dozen,
They answer, "Go to Hell."

We get up early.

Renecito and Tulito are already selling newspapers for *The Miami Times.*

They wait on opposite corners and try to sell papers to the passing cars on *Calle Ocho.*

Renecito has become a master.

He divulges the secret to his success: "Just wait to sell when the traffic light is about to turn green, then you get to keep the change when the customer is forced to drive on."

These newspaper shifts prove to be too scary for Tulito.

The cars drive too perilously close to him.

He often comes home with wet pants.

Papy has at last found a house to rent.

Today we are moving from 9th Street to 4th Street.

This house is a bit roomier.

Carmenchu and her family have moved north to Connecticut in search of work, but there are still twelve of us living together.

We start to assemble what looks like a long conga line down the road.

Some are lugging sofas, some tables.

I bring the lamps and lighter things.

We proceed in single file, singing our *Hymno de la Familia* the entire way to our new house.

While I am walking and singing, I imagine how long it would take to move everything out of CARDECUYOTU.

We had so many people there, countless rooms, loads of toys, heaps of clothes, televisions, a vast multitude of belongings.

"Cuby, hurry up!"

My pace had slowed as my mind wandered back to Havana.

I think of Lu.

She has a way to make everything more fun.

I walk faster.

Up and back on *Avenida SW 22* we go.

We do not have much, but with many of us living together, things add up.

We create our own conga parade.

If Lu was here, she would be dancing in the front, leading the way!

RENY, MAMY, & PAPY — NEW HOME IN MIAMI

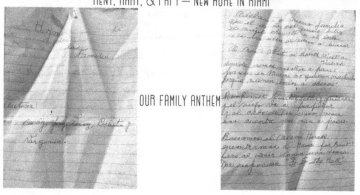

OUR FAMILY ANTHEM

Chapter 53

Ping-Pong

One of my favorite games is ping-pong.
Thanks to the "generosity" of Shenandoah Junior High, we have
    paddles, balls, and a net.
Renecito and Neny "borrowed" the equipment and to our surprise,
    no one asked for it back.
It didn't take long to become professionals!

The dining room table is the perfect size.
We rush home from school at 2:00.
Today I am in a match against Chuchin.
I win handily.
My speedy reflexes help me advance to the championship round.

"Tengo que poner la mesa." Carmita has to set the table.

I don't care for Carmita. I don't think anyone in the family does.
Chucho married her after his wife Hortensia (Tensy and Chuchin's
    mother) had died.
She thinks all the makeup she wears makes her look pretty, but she
    isn't fooling anyone.

Plus, she brought her dog, Chichon, a pudgy dachshund, to *la finca*
    once. He killed my pet chicken Pito.

Later that year, I didn't even feel bad when I heard Chichon was
run over by a car at our beach house in Tarara.
Serves him right.
It was the first time I felt the satisfaction of revenge.

Carmita's only household chore is to set the table.
She loathes that we use it for ping pong.
It is a daily fight between us.
When she announces it's time to ready the table, just like that our
game is over.
I think to myself, why does the table need to be set at 3:00?
I am infuriated.

I go to the bathroom to wash for dinner.
The smell is so bad it almost knocks me out.
Virginia!
Virginia is Abuela's friend who was our neighbor in La Víbora.
She had no place to stay when she arrived in Miami, so of course
we opened our door to her.
Her son Pepin had flown to Miami earlier, alone, and was sent to
live in Montana with an American family.
Everyone knows that after Virginia has been in the bathroom, the
entire house needs to be evacuated, sanitized, and fumigated.
Today, the stench is exceptionally horrific.
After I open the door, a small waft of foul-smelling air escapes and
infiltrates the kitchen.

Even Abuela, who is not known to have a keen sense of smell, looks
up from her cooking, wrinkles her nose, and says, "*Hay, pero
que peste!*" What a stink!

I see Neny laughing from the porch, his nose stuffed with cotton.
Neny would sometimes walk around with cotton balls stuffed up
his nostrils.
This kept him safe from Virginia's stink, and he avoided smelling
Chucho's fishy aroma.
Even at a safe distance, he takes proactive measures.
The cotton ball idea is pretty ingenious, I think.

But I am fuming at Neny.
He knew I was entering ground zero and did not warn me.
I will get him back.
The odor has just about cleared.
Our house is airing out with all the windows open.

Then ... Chucho arrives.
As always the smell of fish exudes from his body after work.
We all insist he leave his clothes outside.
He goes directly to the bathroom to shower.
I think about putting Chucho's shirt under Neny's pillow, but since
he shares a room with the others, I decide I will get my revenge
another way.

I hide all the cotton balls.

TENSY & RENY

Chapter 54

Carnaval

Just the word *Carnaval* makes my blood rush. In an ever-changing Cuba, I still can hold onto *Carnaval*. It excites and transforms me, and brings me back to my African roots. As nights descend, the *Malecón* becomes heaven on Earth. Colorful masks let you be whoever you want, and street vendors' food bursts with flavor. The ear-splitting *corneta china* sounds and the conga begins — the *arrollar*. The *Malecón* becomes a sea of rhythmically moving hot bodies. I am enthralled, captivated by the sounds of the drums. I am one with the music. Extravagant floats pass, each more outrageous than the last. They are exquisitely decorated with flowers and feathers. On the street men in masks move alongside women dancing in racy, colorful outfits adorned with sequins and tassels. It is one of the happiest events of my life, and it comes every year. Every year I look forward to *Carnaval* and dancing the conga. There is nothing like it!

Chapter 55

Darker Than a Wolf's Mouth

Cubans crowd Miami.

More and more of us are coming.

We all need jobs.

In all its generosity, the American government has set up relocating programs.

They are bringing Cubans willing to work to many parts of the U.S.A. and offering jobs and housing.

Carmenchu's father Cuco had the opportunity to go.

They relocated to Bridgeport, Connecticut, an old industrial city in the northeast.

A Jewish landowner who had survived Auschwitz owns garden apartments on Chestnut Avenue, called Chestnut Gardens.

He has offered to help.

He provided Carmenchu's family with a nice rent-free, two-bedroom, two-story apartment.

Carmenchu wrote and told me it was a huge deal when they arrived in Bridgeport.

Even the Mayor, Mayor Tedesco, met them at the airport.

Cuco has convinced Papy to move there.

He says there is an abundance of factories and many jobs.

Papy boards the Greyhound bus.

There is no way *El Camello* could make that trip.

Mamy has packed a shoebox full of cheese sandwiches for his trip.

Another goodbye.
I can feel our fun times are running out.
The family is splitting up again.

Papy is staying with Carmenchu's family on a cot.
He will send for us when he saves enough money to get us there.
Miami will be a memory soon.

He rapidly finds work at the Rockwell factory.
He does not like the work, but he must provide for us.
All the workers, mostly immigrants themselves, laugh at him, berate him, and humiliate him.
A former judge, now he must sweep iron scraps off the floor to feed his family.
He gets paid on Thursdays.

I receive another letter from Carmenchu.
She tells me she loves Thursdays.
She calls them Rockwell Thursdays, because Papy always comes home with a gallon of chocolate ice cream.

We are a proud group.
We make our own way in this new country.
All boys who are able get jobs.
No job is too bad.
Judges turn to sweepers.
Teachers work in assembly lines.
My father writes to us, "Connecticut is darker than a wolf's mouth."
He has saved enough to get us flights to Connecticut.
Instead of greeting more family, we say goodbye to many in the terminal.

Conga & Lu

We miss my Aunt Yolanda and Uncle René by a day.
They arrive from Cuba with their dog, Pinocho, the day after we
  leave Miami.

It is my second time flying in an airplane.
This time, I am not as excited.
I am flying farther from my homeland and leaving more of what
  I have grown to know behind.
I am headed for the unknown once again.
We are taking Allegheny Airlines to Bridgeport.
We have a stopover in Washington, D.C.

Mamy gives me something to eat.
A strange, juicy, peach-colored fruit called cantaloupe.
I wish it were a mango.
I remember fighting over mangos in Cuba.
Their sweet sticky nectar dripping down my neck, the tiny
  hairs sticking in between my teeth as I suck every last bit of
  deliciousness from the pit — delicious.
But today it's cantaloupe.
I hope we don't get cantaloupe tomorrow.

We arrive hours later in Connecticut.
We exit the plane from the back, under where the luggage is kept.
Mamy says this is an unusual way to leave an aircraft.
She jokes that we are exiting out of the "*culo*" (the butt) of the airplane.
"The only way from here is up," she laughs.
I'm thinking maybe Papy could only afford the cheap tickets.

Chucha and Cuco once again welcome us into their small home.
We set up more cots in the living room.
Chuchin, Abuela, and Tensy join us soon after.

Chestnut Gardens has lots of greenery.

There are paths and grass that lead to the other apartments.

We become friends with the other five Cuban families who also stay here.

The Sanchez family in the home behind us have three children, all our same ages.

What luck!

Maria Sanchez must be the most beautiful girl I have ever seen.

I want to grow my hair long like hers.

PAPY IN CONNECTICUT

WASHINGTON DC — LAYOVER

RENY, CUBY, CUQUITO & CARMENCHU

Chapter 56

Mrs. Campbell

I am really missing the amazing dinners and restaurants we would
go to in downtown Havana.
Since coming to America, we have not eaten out.
Papy calls Mamy "Mrs. Campbell."
The extent of much of her cooking is emptying the all-too-familiar
tin can of soup.
She never had to cook in Cuba — it was always Frijolito, Lu, or
Abuela.
She tries her best, but even she admits that she is no Betty Crocker.

Looking up, the stars are hidden.
The ugly factories and clouds of smoke hide them.
I miss the Cuban skies where nearly every constellation was visible.

Neny gets a job as a paperboy.
I work as a babysitter.
Mamy is employed in a factory with Aunt Chucha, making felt
Christmas ornaments and decorations.
Papy works all day at Rockwell and goes to school at night.
He enrolled at Southern Connecticut State College, where he will
get a degree in Education.
Although he already has several doctorates and degrees from the
University of La Habana, a degree in Cuban law is not useful
here in America.

After a draining day at the factory, he takes the bus nightly to the
university to earn another college degree.
He does this with very minimal English skills.
He knows education is the key to success.
Papy has learned a little more than "I've been working on the
railroad" now.

Connecticut has changed something inside me.
My confidence is shattered.
I do not feel that I am the best anymore.
I am embarrassed of my house, my English, and my parents.

We go to Leavitt's Department Store to buy the uniform for my
new school, St. Augustine.
It is a Catholic school.
We receive financial aid to attend, and we pay five dollars a week
for tuition.
"Good morning. It's a beautiful day," the woman says as we pass
her on the sidewalk.
It is a strange expression to us.
In Cuba, no one says it's beautiful out, because every day the
weather is perfect.

I look around.
I guess it is a beautiful day.
Most Connecticut days have been cold and gray.
It is still chilly, but the sun is out, and I can see bits of blue emerging
from the clouds.
I am excited.
These will be the first new clothes I have bought since Cuba.
Everything we would get from *El Refugio* was secondhand.

I don't even mind that it is a uniform.

Lu is not here to help iron it and starch it.

Maybe it will be more comfortable.

Mamy and I take the escalator upstairs.

We make our way to the sign that reads "St. Augustine."

In our broken English, we try to explain to the clerk that we would
    like to purchase a uniform.

"No, no, no," she says.

"Yes, yes, yes," we say.

"No, no, no," she tells us again.

"What is wrong with her?" we say to each other in Spanish.

"This is the Chubbette Department," she says. "You are way too
    thin for these."

We don't know what Chubbette means or understand what she
    has told us.

But needless to say, the uniform that I was so excited to get, I don't
    even want anymore.

The saleswoman makes us feel stupid.

My first new clothes in over a year and instead of buying them we
    leave ridiculed.

We will come back tomorrow to buy it.

Hopefully she will have the day off.

We are all very nervous as we watch JFK dealing with the Cuban
    Missile Crisis.

The USSR and the USA are both close to launching nuclear attacks
    and Cuba is in the middle of it.

The world is on the verge of World War III.

And I still don't have a uniform.

CUBY, RENY, MAMY

RENY
CUBY
MAMY
PAPY

MAMY

Chapter 57

My Name

I went from love to hate.

Cuba, a name I bore proudly, now became my menacing nemesis.

A name that symbolized family, country, and love has forever changed.

My Abuela Cuba told my mother, "Cubita, you carry the name of your mother and your country. Keep these two loves always on a high pedestal."

Mamy chose to give that name to me, too.

I used to cherish it, but I don't anymore.

"What's your name?" I am asked.

In my broken English I reply, "Cuba."

"No, not where you are from, your NAME?" they say loudly, as if I was hard of hearing.

I reply again, stressing both syllables, "CU-BA."

"No, you don't understand," they say, and it goes on and on again and again with almost everyone I meet.

I feel like a fool the minute I open my mouth.

They think I am an idiot who can't answer a simple question.

I wish I could be a Susie or a Jane.

If my olive skin, accent, or clothing didn't give it away, my name sure did.

I am an outsider.

If I could just blend in, belong, and be "normal."

What luck to be stuck with the name Cuba.

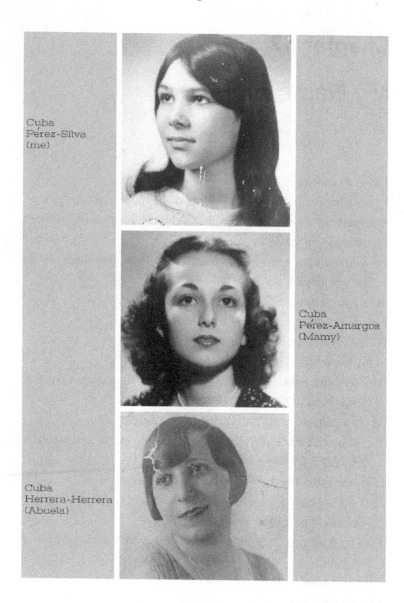

Cuba
Pérez-Silva
(me)

Cuba
Pérez-Amargos
(Mamy)

Cuba
Herrera-Herrera
(Abuela)

Chapter 58

Golden Hill

Chucha and Cuco add baby Beatriz to the family.
I have a new cousin.
We don't have much to bring when I meet her for the first time.
I decide to give her Henry.
I hope she loves him as much as I did.

Space is even tighter now in Chestnut Gardens.
Abuela shares a room with Tensy and Carmenchu.
Without Abuela Cuba here, this family would never survive.
Whatever we need, she always finds a way to supply it.
She is our silent hero.
Cuco and Chucha share a room with Bibi, the new baby, and
    Cuquito.

Soon we are able to move to our own place.
Chuchin comes with us.
Our new home is a horrible apartment on the fourth floor of an
    old brick building on Golden Hill Street.
There is nothing golden about it.
There is only one teeny bedroom where the four of us sleep.
Chuchin sleeps on the couch in living room.
We share one tiny bathroom, but at least Virginia is not here.

I hate it here.

The building is built like a Cuban *solar,* but there is no music, no
life, no joy.

Just a creepy tenement house.

I am always the first to get home from school.

I am frightened to be there alone.

I enter our apartment.

The phone rings.

I hear heavy breathing.

I quickly hang up.

Someone is watching me.

I don't want to tell Mamy or Papy.

I don't want to worry them.

I go to sleep.

I have horrible nightmares.

I am on my way home from school again.

I see our tall dark building.

I sprint up the four flights of stairs.

I make it inside.

I lock the door, bolt it, then pull the gold chain across to latch it.

I make sure the fire escape ladder is pulled up.

The phone rings.

My heart beats out of control.

I don't answer this time.

I turn my record player on to its maximum volume and start to
sing along with Leslie Gore, "It's my party and I'll cry if I want
to, cry if I want to, cry if I want to …."

Next I put on my favorite, "I Will Follow Him," by Dusty Springfield.
I sing "my true love, my true love, my true love."

I hear keys in the door.
Mamy is home from her new job at Catholic Charities for the
Diocese of Bridgeport.
She loves working, but her work doesn't end when she gets home.
She doesn't even put her pocketbook down.
She begins to dance and begins singing in her terrible English, "ma
chula, ma chula, ma chula." I'm not sure Dusty would even
know she was singing her song.
Her English is still not quite there.
I laugh and dance with Mamy and soon my fears fade.

We are still united as a family.
Every Sunday we go to Chucha's for Abuela's *arroz con pollo*
(chicken and rice).
I think there is way more arroz than pollo, but the tradition
remains.
We buy McCall's paper sewing patterns.
Abuela hand-sews the same dress for me, Tensy, and Carmenchu,
but in different colors.
Mine is always yellow.
We listen to Doris Day and Perry Como.

We have lived in Golden Hill for two years.
Mamy was so excited to get a box that Abuelo Delio had shipped
to us.
He sent many old photos from Cuba.
Right away she placed many in frames and hung them all over the
apartment.

I also get a letter from Lu.
There are so many things I wish I could tell her.
Writing each other just isn't enough.
I miss her smile.
I miss her crispy plantains.
I miss the way she would take my hand in hers.
I miss hearing her voice first thing in the morning.
I miss everything about her.
There is a hole left in my heart that only Lu can fill.

We furnish our home from items we buy from the secondhand
 shops.
It is hard to imagine my mother having to shop there.
In Havana, she had the finest and most beautiful furnishings
 I have ever seen.
They were fit for a palace.

Today the newspaper is coming to interview us about how we, as
 Cuban Refugees, came to be living in Connecticut.
Mamy makes our apartment look as good as she can.
On our coffee table is the interior glass of an American coffee
 maker.
She thinks it is a flower vase and fills it with water and carnations.
It is one of the many items she has purchased at the thrift store.
The journalist from *The Bridgeport Post* snaps a picture of us on
 the couch to include with his story.
How embarrassing that all of Bridgeport will see our "vase" once
 the photo is printed with the article.

Poor Mamy, the only coffee makers she knows are the Cuban
 espresso coffee makers that she puts on the stove.

CUBY, ABUELA, MAMY, NENY

Former Cuban Judge Now Living Here Escaped Country By Bluffing Guard

CUBAN LAWYER AND FAMILY—Rene Perez Amargos, a refugee of Castro's Cuba, finds consolation in having his family together in America. With Mr. Amargos in his Bridgeport apartment are, from left, his son, Rene; his daughter, Cuba; and his wife, also Cuba. Mr. Amargos, and a nephew, Delio Silva.

HENRY (MY DOLL)

235

Chapter 59

Monogrammed Handkerchiefs

My life is blessed. I fell in love and now have a little girl. I am sad her father does not take a role in her life, but we manage. Barbara came into my world on a steamy day in June 1962. She is mischievous, daring, and sweet. She reminds me of my dear Conga. The way she talks, the way she walks, the way she acts.

Although times are different, we do not want for anything. We are all given a ration card that allows us to buy basic goods like rice, sugar, and matches. It is called the *libreta de abastecimiento*. This is what we use to get our food, soap, and other living supplies. The amount of food I get for my family is meager. Rations are small, but Abuelo Delio keeps our dining room table filled. I don't know how he manages it. He even makes sure that every Friday Barbara's favorite treat, bonbons, are delivered for her. He gets her every flavor – coffee, nut, malt, cream. She loves them all.

He has become our savior. "Iluminada, you and your family will always be taken care of, as long as I am alive," he tells me. In this time of uncertainty, I somehow feel secure.

Barbara visits with Delio. She calls him Yeyo. Every day from sun up to sundown, they sit and read and rock on the front porch for hours. Sometimes, it seems like she comes home only to shower and sleep. Barbara and Yeyo share a loving bond. They are inseparable. When Barbara came down with the mumps, so did Yeyo. Yeyo spoils Barbara to no end. Recently he threw another extravagant birthday party for her, almost as elaborate and festive as Conga's parties used to be. He bought her a piñata, a doll, and a play kitchen. We had *bocaditos* and a delicious cake with lots of flowers made from icing.

I bring money into our small household by taking on sewing jobs. I am handy with the needle and known around the *barrio* for high-quality work. It is fun and keeps me busy and creative, while I attend to Barbara's needs. I love to sew clothing for her, too. I often get compliments on how well she is dressed. "She looks like a little doll," my mother always tells me when we visit. She is always dressed beautifully.

As I am preparing for bed, Barbara says to me, "Mama, I want to get Yeyo a surprise for his birthday. Can you sew some handkerchiefs for him? Yeyo always has a hankie in his pocket," she says. I tell her it's a great idea.

I stay up late. Using the white material I have, I create handkerchiefs and hand-

237

embroider an "S" for Silva on each one. In the morning I show her the finished products. She is thrilled. They look fabulous. "He will love them!" she says. We find some newspaper and wrap the birthday present with red ribbon that I have saved from the boxes of bon bons. Barbara says red is his favorite color. I can already feel the joy that it will bring to him.

LU
&
ELENA

BARBARA

LU & BARBARA

Chapter 60

St. Augustine

St. Augustine's Cathedral is next to its school.

Our school consists of grades kindergarten through grade eight.

There are two classes of each grade.

It is run by the Sisters of Mercy, with Father O'Connell as our
  principal.

The convent and rectory are on the premises.

Sixth grade has the only lay teacher.

She is the worst of the worst.

It is my luck to have her this year.

The rest of the teachers are nuns.

Neny has Sister Mary Louise.

Neny and I hate going to this school.

The same kids and families stay throughout the nine years here,
  and they all know each other well.

We are the only new kids — the outsiders.

When our parents leave for work, instead of going in, Neny and
  I go into the cathedral.

We find a pew and sit.

When we hear the bell ring to start class, we wait a bit and then
  we bolt.

We cross Washington Avenue to Golden Hill.

We skip the entire day of school.

Chuchin has it much tougher.
He goes downtown to a big public high school, Central High.
It has a very diverse student body.
He tells us a group of bullies meet him outside of school and
    demand his lunch money or they threaten to beat him up daily.
No wonder he is so skinny.

Today I know I must go to class.
Mrs. Collins is my teacher.
Mrs. Collins will never be in contention for any sort of teaching
    award.
She is a true witch.
She must be the coldest, least nurturing teacher in the world.
She has no idea how to teach children, especially those who are
    just learning English.
She calls my name.
She makes me go to the board and diagram sentences.
I don't even know what that means.
I have never even learned English grammar, EVER.
I suffer trying to make a sentence of those designs with words the
    other kids put on the board.
I turn as red as Mamy's lipstick.
I fail miserably.
Mrs. Collins orders me to sit down.
Hours pass and I can't wait any longer.
I raise my hand and stand by my desk.
I ask, "Can I go to the bathroom please?"
"What did you say!" she screeches.
I ask again and again, feeling ridiculed and unsure why she makes
    me keep repeating myself.
By now others are laughing.

She finally says with a sly and nasty smirk, "Yes, you CAN go the
bathroom. Yes, you have the ability to go to the bathroom,
BUT in the United States you must use the word MAY for
permission. Yes, you MAY go to the bathroom."

I run to a stall.
My Chubbette uniform skirt, which is way too big for me, is
already a tiny bit wet.
I will never ask to use the restroom ever again.

I sit in class staring out the wall of windows.
I start to see white specks.
The specks turn to flakes.
It is snowing!
I have never seen snow before.
It is beautiful.
I want to run outside and touch it.
"Cuba," Mrs. Collins says, "come up to the board."
Oh no. Here we go again.

At recess, we go to the parking lot and jump rope.
I have a few friends.
I miss the sports from Miami and Cuba.
No sports here.
Papy got me a sled, and we went ice skating at the pond.
The boys play with baseball cards.
I try out for the only thing available.
The church choir.
They accept me, and we practice daily.
We sing at the ten o'clock mass on Sundays.
I learn every word of every song.

We walk home from school with the Sanchez kids.
Up Pequonock Street, and on the way back, we stop at the small
    variety candy store called Pops.
All the walkers come here to buy treats after school.
I long for a *pirulí*.

We stop daily, but Neny and I can never buy.

Saint Augustine Cathedral School

CHUBETTE UNIFORM

Chapter 61

School Lunches

It's early Saturday morning in Bridgeport.

Neny is on his paper route.

We walk to the butcher shop on Main Street with Papy to buy our big ham for five dollars.

Unlike the store in Havana, there are no live animals.

We enter the massive freezer and pick our meat.

Definitely not as fresh as in Cuba.

Mamy makes us our lunches for school.

After she found out that Chuchin was being bullied and his lunch money stolen daily, he gets Mamy's lunches, too.

Lunches are always the same — a ham sandwich.

That ham has to last all week, so they are very thin sandwiches.

We also buy a carton of milk for five cents from school.

Lunch time is at 11:45.

I go to the coat room to get my paper bag.

It is easy to spot.

All my classmates have shiny lunchboxes.

Mine is the only bag.

I go back to my desk and take out my lunch.

Everyone is talking about their food, trading snacks and treats.

No one wants anything I have.

Conga & Lu

I am embarrassed about my lunch.
I see kids take their packages of Hostess or TastyCake cupcakes out.
They all contain two or three cupcakes.
I unwrap the wax paper containing my single cake.
Mamy would open the package at home and separate them into
    individual servings.
Neny, Chuchin, and I would each get only one.

At least it's not Friday.
Fridays we can't eat meat.

Fridays mean egg sandwiches.

CARMENCHU, TENSY, CUBY, YOLY

RENY & CUBY

Chapter 62

JFK

I sit in Sister Gilmary's seventh grade classroom.
She is an angel put on Earth.
The chalkboard says November 22, 1963.
We have just finished lunch.

I hear an announcement on the intercom.
"President Kennedy has been shot."
We are frozen, and then come the cries, the tears.
Sister Gilmary prays with us.
She tells us we will get through this as a nation, with God's help.
She gives each of us a loving hug and we are sent home.
Mamy is already there crying.

We sit in silence and watch the news coverage.
Today, we don't fight over which channel to watch.

TV is always a bone of contention at our house.
The small black-and-white console with rabbit ears is always the
    source of bitter fights.
There are only three TV channels.
I like to watch *The Adventures of Rocky and Bullwinkle*.
Chuchin likes Westerns.
Neny likes junk.
We always fight to see who gets to see their show.

Last week, in a moment of meanness, Chuchin and I were fighting
over what channel.
I said, "Well this is MY house, so I get to choose."
I felt very bad.
I guess it has been building up in me, having to share everything.

Mamy must have overheard, because the next day she had made
up a schedule.
Chuchin had Mondays, Neny had Tuesdays, and I had Wednesdays.
Then the order was repeated again.
All afternoon that Friday we are glued to the TV crying for John
John and Caroline.
He was their father and our president.
He tried to get Castro out so we could return to Cuba.
He was too young and too smart to die.

Even though it is Friday night, we don't feel like taking our usual walk
to King Cole Supermarket. Normally Chuchin, Neny, and I would
race home to open up the only bag of cookies for the week.
We'd sit and devour the entire bag in two minutes, stuffing
our faces.
But tonight, I don't even feel like eating.
I hope John John gets all the cookies he wants.
I don't think we turned the TV off for a week, watching the news
coverage.
JFK's funeral, LBJ being sworn in as President, Oswald apprehended.
We watch in disbelief as Jack Ruby shoots Lee Harvey Oswald on
live television.
It takes me back.
I remember the executions that were televised in Cuba.
I pray that they have stopped.

Mamy walks around the neighborhood, looking for people sitting
    outside like they had done in Cuba.
She finds no one.
The porches are empty.
As much as I loved Miami, I hate Connecticut.
I am sad, struggling, shy.
Connecticut is the beginning of the end.
All the Silvas go our own ways to make it in this new country.
In Miami, all of us were together.
Now some of us are in Connecticut.
Some have relocated to Philadelphia, some reside in New York,
    some are living in Miami, and Abuelo Delio is all alone in
    Cuba, waiting for the time when we can return.
I have received word from Lu that she is still living at
    CARDECUYOTU.
She has a baby girl.
I miss her so.

I wonder if I will ever make it back to Havana.

SISTER MARY LOUISE
&
CUBY

Chapter 63

Elena

I sit rocking in my chair and use a fan to ease the heat. Being pregnant in this summer heat is not easy. As my body grows, so does the discomfort. I have a feeling I will have another girl. This pregnancy has been very similar to my first one. I was very nauseous the first three months. The next three I was just tired, and now that I am nearing the end, I am just very uncomfortable. Barbara plays with her doll on the floor by my swollen feet. The mailman sees me outside and hands me a letter. I see it is from Matanzas and hurry to open it.

My uncle writes that my mother's health is failing. I rush inside to gather up a few of our belongings and hurry to catch the next bus. I pray that I am in time to see my mother's smiling eyes once more.

Unfortunately, time is not on my side. I am too late. She passed moments before I arrive. We share grief together. A beautiful woman is gone. It is good to hold my family in my arms. God has plans for us all.

Elena is here. I have another baby girl. It has only been two weeks since my mother passed. Elena's eyes remind me of my mother. She is calm, quiet, and content. I just love sitting and holding her. Sorrow has turned to joy. Mothers are miracles.

Chapter 64

I Have a Dream

"I have a dream," his voice booms.

I listen to his words as he speaks to thousands in Washington, D.C.

I am inspired.

Martin Luther King, Jr., is peacefully fighting to end racism.

He is a master.

The words he speaks stay with me and fill me with hope.

Every year in eighth grade, our school has an oration contest.

Everyone must write a speech.

It is a filtering process.

Week after week, students have slowly been weeded out.

We must deliver our speech to an auditorium full of people.

The winner and runner up get prestigious-looking plaques.

This year's theme is free enterprise in America.

I have spent weeks researching and writing my speech at the
    public library.

I am determined to win a plaque.

There are only ten of us left.

I am a finalist.

I stand in front of the audience and try my best to invoke the
    confidence and greatness of Martin Luther King, Jr.

I look out and see my parents sitting in the far back of the
    auditorium.

I begin … and in my heavy accent deliver the speech of a lifetime.
I end with "life, liberty, and the pursuit of happiness."

They are ready to announce the winners …
I hold my breath.
"Runner up: Cuba Pérez-Silva."
I am elated.
They announce that Dennis Vitrella, the class vice president, is
    the winner.
I don't know if they felt bad for me and my broken English or if my
    speech was really that good.

I am happy to be in America where we are free.
I proudly carry my winning plaque home.

My father tacks on one more degree.
He gets a job at St Mary's High School teaching Spanish.
All the Cuban men in the family must have also earned a master's
    degree in bargain shopping.
When burgundy sweaters went on sale last winter, each of my
    uncles and my father ended up modeling them in the streets.
Never mind the awful color, the price was right.
I am convinced that my Uncle Tony may even have a doctorate in
    thriftiness.
He came over one day smoking a cigarette.
"Uncle Tony, I didn't know you smoked," I said to him.
He replied "I don't, but they were selling cartons two for one. It was
    too good a deal to pass up!"

I have spent hours at the public library.
I started in the children's section.

Conga & Lu

I escape into the stories where I can be anywhere and anyone.
Today I am in fiction.
I choose *David Copperfield* by Dickens.

I dream of boys, of friends, and of fitting in.
I also have a dream that one day I will return to Cuba.

Is it only a dream?

TONY, PAPY AND RENE IN THEIR BURGUNDY SWEATERS

257

Chapter 65

Quinceañera

Papy has found us a great apartment on Park Avenue.

I finally have my own room, and it is the biggest one in the house.

I am fifteen!

For my birthday, Papy bought me a beautiful white French provincial bedroom set.

Neny still has the couch.

The Silvas don't celebrate *quinceañeras* with huge outlandish dresses or extravagant affairs.

But they are still celebrated in a significant way.

When girls turn fifteen, we get a small solitaire diamond ring from our parents.

Mamy makes the usual party food.

Abuela makes a cake.

We have *bocadito* sandwiches, chicken and rice, Jell-O, and chicken salad.

Cuban parties always have a lot of food.

The few American get-togethers I have been to are very different.

Usually they are held in a dark basement.

No adults, only teenagers.

They have some chips and soda.

That's it.

Boys and girls dance or make out.

We have a big celebration in our spacious living room.

My whole family comes.

Even those who are not in Connecticut arrive for the fiesta. They travel from New York and Philadelphia.

All of my cousins, aunts, and uncles — young and old.

I invite some high school friends, but I am quickly embarrassed, because my American friends do not party like us.

They look surprised as they see Mamy leading the conga line.

Everyone is speaking Spanish and everyone talks at the same time.

I want to hide.

Mamy and Papy give me my solitaire, but I am embarrassed to wear it.

Papy walks in.

He has arrived home earlier than Mamy today.

With a smile he says, "I have a surprise for you!"

He disappears for a moment then emerges with an adorable brown and black puppy!

It is a German shepherd-collie mix (a real Rin-Tin-Tin/Lassie).

He tells me it reminds him of my Rin-Tin from Cuba.

He rescued him from animal control.

Mamy has made it clear she does not want a dog.

We will call him "Chico," Papy declares.

His name means "boy."

"See!" Papy says, "We don't have a dog, we have another boy!"

I am ecstatic.

I love Chico.

He is perfect.

Lu would love taking him for walks with me.

I wonder who is helping the strays in the park since I have left
Cuba.

Now Papy is the one hiding puppies from Mamy!

CHICO

15TH BIRTHDAY

261

Chapter 66

Brownies

The Beatles want to hold my hand
And Bob Dylan is blowin' in the wind.
I have a portable record player.
Tonito is visiting from New York City.
I love laughing, talking, and dancing with him, just as we had done
    in Havana.
He is always happy.
Cousin Yoly loves dancing too.
She teaches us all the popular Rock and Roll moves.
When those two are together they laugh and laugh.

In Connecticut we leave our refugee status behind.
We drove to Montreal and got to see Niagara Falls.
It was a spectacular sight.
Once we crossed back into New York, we became residents with
    green cards.
I learn to do my own thing.

We have many neighbors in Bridgeport.
My father has nicknames for them all.
The little terror Manuel Antonio, who lives near us, he calls "*coño*"
    (a swear word).
Poor Manuel Antonio can't pronounce his own name, and that is
    what it sounds like when he introduces himself.

"*Pata Larga*" (Long Leg) is Mr. Collins, the stretchy fellow who lives downstairs.

Papy carpools to work with a woman he calls "*Cara Mango*" (Mango Face).

The portly neighbor, Manolo Vega, who has an uncanny ability to knock on our door as soon as Mamy puts the food out for dinner, he calls "*El Pegado*" (the One Who Sticks).

Manolo plops right down at the table with his cigar nearly every night for his free meal then sticks around for dessert.

And then there is Juanito "*Rompe Teclas*" (Break the Keys) who plays the piano so loudly it penetrates through the walls.

We have a whole cast of characters living around us.

Neny has been accepted at Georgetown University. My parents are so proud.

As a refugee, who knew such little English only a few years ago, gaining acceptance to a top American University is no easy feat.

I guess Papy was right he didn't need to waste his time in Americusa's pre-K.

I like to work.

I start babysitting at Chestnut Gardens.

I especially like to babysit for the Americans, because their fridge is always filled with snacks and goodies.

The mom would always say, "Help yourself to anything you want."

The Cuban families never have that great of a snack selection.

A few of us go downtown to Bridgeport's courthouse and receive our Social Security cards.

The Jewish bakery chain Zwerdlings is hiring 15-year-olds.

A lady named Trudy hires me immediately after my interview.

There are so many names of so many pastries that I have never
heard of.

My first customer asks for two cheesecakes.

What is that? I am stumped ....

I have no idea and see no cakes with cheese on them.

She points to two cakes behind the counter.

They look like flan with no caramel.

Who would want a cake with cheese?

Sounds disgusting.

None of the desserts that we sell are familiar to me.

Where are the guava *pasteles*, the *empanadas*, the *yemitas*, the
torticas de morón?

I have a lot to learn.

I find out quickly that the worst part of my job is when the customer
asks for sliced bread.

It is next to impossible to fit the many slices back into the tight bag.

I end up with many loaves on the floor.

Papy drives me to work.

It's the East Main Street location.

There are three excellent bonuses to working here.

First, I have the Sunday 6:00 a.m. shift, so I get to miss Sunday
mass.

Second, I have money and am able to buy things that I want.

I am eyeing a yellow puffy-sleeved dress — only one more dollar
to go.

The third, and the best part of the job, is that I get to eat all the
brownies I want from the back of the bakery.

I feel I will soon become a chubbette if I stay here too much longer.

CROSSING OVER FROM CANADA WITH OUR GREEN CARDS

265

Chapter 67

Vacation

My 22-year-old history teacher Mr. Flynn told us Vietnam is
  getting really bad.
He is joining the Navy for four years.
He is my favorite teacher.
I hope that he gets home safely.

Neny is coming back from Georgetown.
He hitchhikes home all the time, but Mamy sends him back on
  the bus.
Spring in Connecticut is wonderful.
Daffodils begin to bloom.
Dogwoods are beginning to show their beautiful flowers.
I love to see the changing of the seasons.
In Cuba the weather was always warm and sunny.

My heart aches.
Martin Luther King, Jr., was assassinated.
The world has lost a great man.
I have a feeling we're going to have more racial troubles.
The world seems like it is in a state of much conflict.

Abuela Iraida and Abuelo Pompeyo arrived in Miami from Cuba.
It has been six and a half years since I have seen them.
We get tickets right away to go visit them in Miami.

They are staying with my Aunt Gladis, Uncle Luis, and their son
Luis Juan.

They both look very old.

They tell me how beautiful I have grown.

I miss Abuela Iraida's apartment in Cuba.

She shows me her statue of St. Lazarus.

She was able to bring it from Cuba.

There is a candle burning beside it.

Aunt Gladis is six months pregnant.

I sleep on a small bench in the living room.

We go to the beach and catch up with Papy's family.

If I don't go back north with a tan, I don't know what I'll do.

I spend hours in the sun.

My grandparents have changed a lot.

But so have I.

I love Miami.

It is so different than Connecticut.

We head to Mamy's friend Cotona's house for dinner.

Sylvia, the girl I knew as a child in Cuba, is here.

It's nice to see her again!

She tells me all about Cuban boys.

I didn't realize there are so many rules you need to remember if
you want to date a Cuban.

"Cuban boys are quite different than American boys. You can't let
him kiss you until he asks you to be his girlfriend, no good
night kisses," she says.

"You have to act very ladylike and proper with the Cuban boys."

I have only gone out with Americans.

I don't know any Cuban boys in Connecticut, except Joaco Sanchez,
my neighbor, and he's practically my brother.

Miami makes me feel like a beautiful woman.
I only have to walk out of the house, and I get "hellos" and horn beeps.
Cars even stop and yell things like "beautiful" and "sugar pie."
I'm not used to this, but I don't mind it.
Sylvia says that if they honk their horn, they really like you.
And just on one corner I got three beeps, five stares, and one
    "beautiful."

We go into downtown Miami on the bus.
I buy two dresses.
I get one at Jordan Marsh, and it is so sexy.
We take the bus back and I pretend to be an American.

After a few days of the beach and catching up with family, it's time
    to go.
I can't get over my face and body.
It is unbelievable — all swollen, blistered, and bright, bright red.
Sadly, we have to leave all of these tan, blond hunks and head back
    to Connecticut.
At least my hair will not be as curly back home.
The humidity is horrible in Florida.

The airport is crowded.
It's been nearly ten years since I was the frightened little girl
    clutching my doll in this same airport.
I see many sailors.
I pray for their safe return.
The Vietnam War is escalating.
More and more people are losing their lives.

I am looking good wearing my yellow dress, jacket, and hat.

The flight on National on the way home is better than Eastern.
I already miss the warm breeze, the palm trees, and the empanadas.

I can't believe even more sadness has hit America.
Today is June 5th.
I wake up to the television playing "God Bless America."
Senator Bobby Kennedy was shot at around midnight in California.
He is now in very critical condition.

The Kennedys have so much and yet so little.
The bullet struck him in his brain.
He is undergoing surgery now.
It's been over four years since his brother was shot.
I remember crying so much!
I have more tears in my eyes today.
This is the greatest nation in the whole world, and so much is going
    down the drain.
On my way to the bakery, I stop at church to pray for the Kennedys.
I love that family, especially Bobby, John John, and Caroline.

Love is in the air.
Carmenchu is madly in love with her boyfriend Jorge.
Even though they are both Cuban, they met in the United States.
They have fallen in love through letters written back and forth
    from Vietnam to Philadelphia.
Chuchin is engaged to an American girl, Donna — she will be the
    first American to join our family.
Tensy got married to her boyfriend Enrique.
She looked absolutely gorgeous.
We spent hours decorating the reception hall.

Someday it will be my turn.

PAPY

MAMY

MIAMI HUNKS

CUBY, RENY, PAPY

MIAMI BEACH

TENSY'S WEDDING

PAPY, MAMY, ABUELO POMPEYO

Chapter 68

Tattoo

She showed me her left forearm.
As she turned it over, I saw a tattoo.
It was a five-digit number.

"I am also an immigrant. An immigrant who was welcomed
   into the arms of America. I lived and saw horrors in the
   concentration camp at Auschwitz. I am one of the fortunate
   ones that survived to tell the story of how we Jews were
   persecuted. Many of us were put to death by the Nazis."
She spoke solemnly with conviction.
My heart melted.

Mrs. Annie Baum, the Jewish landlady of our new apartment on Park
   Avenue, must be the kindest, most generous soul I have ever met.
She lives next door alone.
She speaks with a heavy accent.
Her basement and attic are filled with fine furnishings and
   household goods.
She said to Papy and Mamy, "Take whatever you need for your
   apartment. You never have to repay me. I once was like you."
Thanks to Mrs. Baum, our new flat became our new castle.
We were able to "borrow" couches, lamps, beds, and tables.
Whenever we needed something, I would go down her back stairs,
   peer into the dark and mysterious basement, and emerge with

newfound goods; never once did I ever hear her complain about injustices.

She is a proud woman with a heart of gold.

She awakened me to a whole new culture — her Jewish culture.

Every Passover she would come to our home with a bottle of Manischewitz wine and matzah crackers.

As I sat with her at her kitchen table and she shared her yummy baked goods.

I stopped feeling sorry for myself.

I stopped wishing I wasn't a refugee and I stopped wishing I was someone else.

Mrs. Baum is strong, brave, and inspirational.

She survived the Holocaust with dignity.

She shares her love and kindness with immigrants like me.

I will never forget her.

Chapter 69

Mixer

It's Friday night.

I finish ringing up the last customer at Korvettes.

I've worked here at E.J. Korvettes Department store all through high school.

It is very steady, and they let me work as much or as little as I want.

My friends are waiting out front to pick me up.

We are going to a mixer.

I go to an all-girls Catholic school.

Thanks to the Ecumenical Council, our freshman year was the first year they separated the boys and girls.

Since there are only girls at school, we are free to discover who we are, to be ourselves, study, and have fun while not trying to impress anyone.

We pretend we ride horseys through the hallways, make hippie headbands from Wonder Bread bags, and pass notes about the boys we would meet up with after school.

At the end of the day when the bell rings, the boys are the first ones waiting for us outside.

We hike our skirts up as high as we can, but if we get caught, the nuns come around with razor blades and quickly cut our hems.

Our skirts end up long and uneven.

The nuns are mean, unhappy, and frustrated.

They seem to take it out on us.

Everyone's favorite is Father Stubbs.

He is our young and handsome guidance counselor.

He gives us passes to see him for "counseling," which consists of drinking sweet mass wine and smoking cigarettes in his office.

We also ride everywhere in his cool convertible sports car.

I don't know how the nuns put up with him, or how he keeps his job, but I am happy he is there.

Junior year, my French teacher fixed me up with a boy she knew named Joe.

She had a young friend who was in the Navy and wanted me to meet him.

We went out and I nicknamed him Oregon Joe.

He was from Eugene, Oregon.

He called way too much.

The phone never stopped ringing.

It was hard to get rid of him.

I wonder why my teacher would fix me, one of her students, up with a sailor?

Mamy and Papy never knew about Oregon Joe.

I give my long brown hair a quick brush, and we pile into Chris' Green Triumph.

Her mom had won the groovy, sporty car in a game show called *Concentration* with Hugh Downs.

The self-proclaimed "boresome foursome" — Phyllis, Donna, Chris, and I — never need dates on Friday nights.

We always have fun whatever we do.

Fairfield University is known to have the best dances.

We are only seniors in high school, but we get in using fake college IDs.

I have it easy.

A quick stop at Woolworths and I transform Neny's Georgetown
ID into my own.

Since René can be a boy or girls' name, I am golden.

I replace my picture and just like that I am a college student.

Since Chris has more brothers and sisters than I have cousins, it is
easy for all the other girls to pretend to be one of them.

At the party they serve us punch and play records.

We have lots of fun dancing and laughing.

We all agree college parties are cooler.

WONDER BREAD HEADBANDS & FR. STUBBS

NOTRE DAME GIRLS HIGH SCHOOL

SENIOR HATS

DONNA   CUBA   DALE

"COUNSELING"   MR. SCOTT

Chapter 70

Senior Prank

"He's coming!!"

We hear his steps approaching the classroom.

Everything is in place.

He walks in.

Anne Schneider drops the needle on the record.

We stand up and begin slowly removing our blazers one button at a time to Gypsy Rose Lee's song.

We then swing our jackets over our heads and drop them to the floor.

Mr. Scott, who is extremely shy and can't maintain eye contact, bolts out the door.

The burlesque dance we had planned barely got started ... we didn't even get to the blouses.

The carefully laid-out intention was to strip down to our bikinis but our plan didn't work.

Our teacher left the class running in search of Mother Superior, Sister Joan.

We are suspended for the last week of our senior year, banned from all the planned fun senior activities — the trip to D.C., our nation's capital; class parties; and picnics.

Mamy and Papy cried, "How could you do this to us?"

They go to the convent and plead and cry some more until the nuns decide to forgive us.

We miss many events, but they do permit us to walk in the
graduation ceremony.

The rest of our senior class stood behind us and said in unison that
if we didn't walk they wouldn't either.

I feel sad for Mamy and Papy.

It was a joke that did not turn out as planned, but we all agree it
was worth it.

The look on Mr. Scott's face was worth a million bucks.

Sometimes young, good, Catholic girls do mean things.

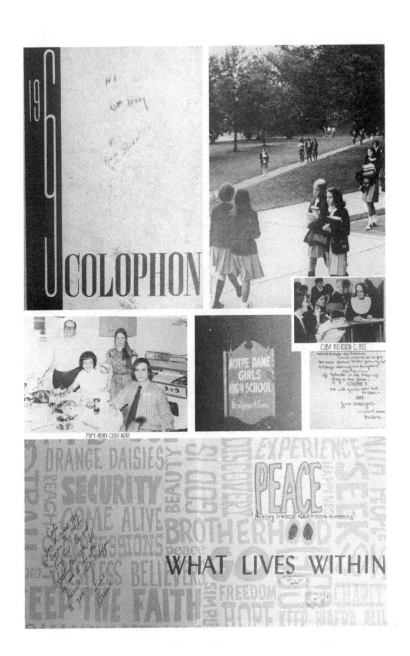

COLOPHON

CUBY RELIGION CLASS

PRPY-MAMY-CUBY-NENY

ORANGE DAISIES
SECURITY
COME ALIVE
EXPERIENCE
PEACE
BROTHERHOOD
WHAT LIVES WITHIN
KEEP THE FAITH

279

Chapter 71

Summer of Love

"He wants to ask you out!" my friend Jeanie says excitedly. "If he
    does, will you say yes?"
"BRIAN?" I ask. "Brian Giblin wants to ask me out?"

I have known Brian since I was a freshman.
I remember the first day I saw him — he was at cheer practice.
Afterward, we all piled into Dave's car to go to the mall.
There were probably ten of us in there.
Cagg told Brian to sit on her lap.
He said "no," and squeezed in next to me.
He took my notebook which was covered in daisies.
I had doodled and written my name all over it.
When he got out, he smiled and said, "Bye, Cuba."
He knows my name now, I thought.
He is just so gorgeous.

Brian is a year older than me and went to Notre Dame Boys High
    School, but now he goes to Sacred Heart University.
Brian is the most popular and the handsomest boy I know.
Everyone knows Brian had gone out with Missy, he had gone out
    with Charlene, and many, many others.
I wonder, why me?
I remember when I first met him, I thought, "I like him but I will
    never chase him. He'll come to me if he wants me."

"OF COURSE!" I tell Jeannie, whose brother is good friends with
    Brian.
He calls me the next day.

It is Sunday, May 11th, Mother's Day.
We no longer wear matching dresses, but we walk to mass together.
We walk back home and are just finishing lunch.
"We aren't doing anything else today, right?" I ask.
"No, *mi hija*. Why?" Mamy responds.
"A boy named Brian asked me to go for a picnic. Can I go?"
"OK," Mamy says. "Take your brown sweater. It is windy."
I put on my feathered earrings and my suede headband.

Brian borrows his brother's car.
We go to 90 Acres Park on Park Avenue.
Hours pass.
We spend time finding rocks, talking, sitting, eating.
It's perfect.
He is cool, confident, and charismatic.
I am enthralled with his presence.
It's that easy.
We fall in love.

It's time for me to go.
I have to get home.
I wasn't sure Brian would even show up, so I didn't cancel my plans
    with my boyfriend, Kenny.
I have just enough time to change out of my bell-bottoms and into
    my long blue skirt with the matching top.
I pull my hair back into a long low ponytail and tie a scarf around it.
I take off my headband.

Kenny is at the door.
We leave quickly.
I tell him about Brian, and he knows that he has lost me.

I get back home and am still euphoric over my afternoon with Brian.
I already know Brian will be the one I marry.
As I am writing "Mrs. Cuba Giblin" all over my diary, Mamy
    comes in my room and gives me my pocketbook.
"Brian dropped this off for you," she says.
"I don't think he is friends with Kenny," Papy adds.

While I am over the moon about Brian, Neil Armstrong actually
    walked on the moon.
This summer is shaping up to be great.

It's the concert of the century, and Brian has tickets.
All of our favorites are playing.
Arlo Guthrie, CCR, Janis Joplin, Jefferson Airplane.
It will be so far out.
"Woodstock?" Papy says. "New York? Hippie music festival? NO
    way, Cuby, you are not going."
So many friends of mine got to go.
My strict Cuban parents do not allow it.
What a bummer.
They don't understand how things are in America.

Don't they know this is the summer of love?

CUBA PEREZ-SILVA

Souvenir Prom Photograph

CUBA & BRIAN

283

Chapter 72

Baseball

Baseball is the most loved and popular sport in Cuba. My father and brothers always enjoyed both watching and playing. My father called baseball the heart of Cuba. Shortly after the revolution, Fidel Castro disbanded the Cuban League and replaced professional baseball with a new amateur league in 1962. Now we watch during the cooler months as sixteen teams from all over the island play each other. We are fans of the *Industriales de la Habana*. The Lion is their mascot.

No one is a bigger fan than Yeyo. He goes to several games a month and often takes Barbara. Today, he takes us all along. The *Estadio Latinoamericano* is grand. It used to be called *Estadio del Cerro*. We sit in the stands with thousands of other spectators. Like all things, the ball park is owned by the government.

It is very different from the baseball fields used in Matanzas. Our local field was not in great shape. The grandstand was in desperate need of a paint job, and chicken wire was put up as fencing. Even though it wasn't fancy, it was always full. Sometimes as a girl, I would have to stand outside the sidelines and watch, since all the seats would be taken by the factory workers and cane cutters who would pile into the stands to let loose and enjoy themselves after a long hard day of work.

We chant, "Go, Lions!" Yeyo gets my children blue flags, which they wave as the pep band plays. We have great seats. The energy is high. With a few more wins they will go to the championships.

The Lions are wearing their all-blue uniforms today, since they are the home team. They are playing the *Naranjas de Villa Clara*. They have yellow jerseys and black pants. We sit in a sea of blue. Our seats are behind first base. The bat cracks the ball, and it sails into the air. It comes closer and closer and I move for fear it may hit me. I tell Yeyo to duck but I am too late. The foul ball strikes his right ear. Blood drips onto his shirt. I quickly take his handkerchief and apply pressure to the wound. The white hanky is soon red. I use one of the fabric flags that Elena is waving. It slows the bleeding. Yeyo refuses to leave the game. "Go, Lions!" he yells and smiles.

We all continue watching knowing that he is in good spirits. The *Industriales* win! 6-4! We arrive home to find a letter waiting for us from Conga. What a wonderful surprise!

"DEAR LU: IT'S BEEN SO LONG THAT I HAVE BEEN WAITING TO WRITE THIS LETTER THAT NOW THAT I AM DOING IT I DON'T KNOW HOW TO BEGIN OR WHAT TO WRITE. I IMAGINE THAT YOU WILL HAVE TO SIT FOR A LONG WHILE SO THAT YOU CAN REMEMBER WHO IS WRITING YOU THIS LETTER. I HOPE YOU REMEMBER SOMETHING ABOUT ME. I HAVE ALWAYS THOUGHT OF YOU DURING THESE YEARS AND THE TRUTH IS THAT IT'S BEEN MANY YEARS. I AM 18 YEARS OLD AND I HAVE CHANGED A LOT JUST LIKE EVERYONE CHANGES. IN SEPTEMBER I WILL GO TO THE UNIVERSITY AND LIVE THERE BECAUSE IT IS FAR FROM HOME. NENY WILL SOON TURN TWENTY AND IS IN THE UNIVERSITY IN WASHINGTON. HE IS STUDYING MEDICINE. PAPY AND MAMY ARE DOING GREAT — A TINY BIT OLDER BUT YOU CAN'T TELL .

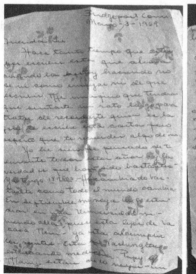

AND HOW ARE YOU LU? I HOPE YOU ARE AS GOOD AS YOU WERE WHEN I LEFT YOU. AND YOUR NEW LITTLE DAUGHTER? WELL SHE MUST BE NEARING HER SEVENTH BIRTHDAY. I HAVE NOT MUCH TO TELL ABOUT LIFE HERE. LIFE IS VERY DIFFERENT HERE AS COMPARED TO THE LIFE IN CUBA. I DON'T KNOW IF I CAN ASSIMILATE TO THE CUBAN LIFE AGAIN BECAUSE HAVING GROWN UP HERE IT'S THE ONLY THING I KNOW. I LOVE IT HERE. I AM GOING TO SCHOOL AND I WORK AT A STORE AT NIGHT. OH LU PLEASE WRITE TO ME AND TELL ME ABOUT YOU AND YOUR LIFE. YOU TRULY HAVE BEEN A VERY SPECIAL PERSON IN MY LIFE AND I WOULD LIKE TO RENEW OUR FRIENDSHIP. MY ADDRESS IS ..."

Chapter 73

Mongoose Juice

I will attend college in the fall, but we get to spend the summer
together.

We are both working.

I work at a factory that makes plastic packing baggies.

I also still work Korvettes from 6:00 to 10:00 at night.

Brian works at a trucking company.

He also paints with his brothers when he can.

I meet his family.

They are a big Irish bunch.

His sisters are all married.

He is the youngest of seven.

The baby.

His brothers are fun.

His sisters are sweet and loving.

The Silvas are known to be cold, some would say stuck up.

Not the Giblins.

They are warm, friendly, and happy.

The women are beer-drinking angels.

I had never seen a woman drink a beer before going to his sister's
house.

Mary warns me to watch out for her baby brother, Brian.

"We like you," Nancy says to me.

"Treat her well," they tell Brian.

Brian's mother died when he was young.

His father was a hardworking immigrant from Ireland.

He later developed an alcohol problem, which caused health issues
and problems with the family.

Brian and his brother Billy rent a house together in Bridgeport.

No parents.

The teenage Giblin boys always have the best shindigs.

They work hard and play hard.

My friends come and we all drink the Mongoose Juice.

It tastes awful but makes everyone happy.

Brian is always the life of the party.

I hop on the back of his motorcycle.

I wrap my arms around him and we are off.

He parks the motorcycle down the block and walks me to my door.

My parents would NEVER let me on a motorcycle.

I know they think he is not good for me.

I have to do a lot of lying to be with him.

I am unsure where to go to college.

Georgetown, Boston, the University of Connecticut?

Brian wants me to stay in Connecticut.

He wants to get engaged soon.

More than anything, I want to be married and have a family.

I ask my father why I even need to go to college.

"Go get your degree and keep it in your back pocket," he tells me.

He is working at St. Mary's High School and also has become a
professor at Sacred Heart University.

Papy says, "Your mind is your best weapon. Arm it with as much
knowledge as you can."

Papy must be ready for war.

I can't even keep up with the number of degrees he has.

It's moving day.
We only have one car, since none of Brian's cars last long.
I have lost track of how many he has wrecked.
Mamy, Papy, Neny, and Brian have helped me fit all that I can into
    Papy's VW bug.
I can't take too much.
Mamy has sewn cloth nametags inside all my clothes.
Even my bras and panties.
I pack the same *croqueta* bag I brought with me from Cuba.
Instead of Henry, I take my Raggedy Ann Doll with me.

My parents love Brian now.
They know he is a bit of a rebel, not a good Cuban boy, but realize
    that my heart belongs to him.
He can make anything, fix anything, and solve everything.

After settling into my freshman dorm compound, the Jungle, I am
    officially a college student at UConn.
I can retire my fake ID.
My classes are all in the morning.
I enjoy the college atmosphere.
I am an activist around campus.
The Vietnam War is taking all our boys and many are not
    coming back.
I want Nixon to hear our voices.
Cousin Chuchin joined the Army right after high school.
Carmenchu's and Tensy's boyfriends Jorge and Enrique are
    drafted as well.

I pray they are safe.

BRIAN'S BIKE

CUBA & BRIAN

DORM ROOM UCONN

CROQUETTA FROM CUBA

PACKED FOR COLLEGE

THE JUNGLE

Chapter 74

Changing Faces of CARDECUYOTU

"Mama, there are new people moving into Yeyo's house!" Barbara comes to the backyard, where I sit sewing her a dainty pink dress under the shade of the mamey tree. I stand up and open the back door. "Yes," I reply. "The empty bedrooms will no longer be empty."

A few years ago, new tenants were moved into the upstairs. A young couple, Elda and her husband, now live in Carmenchu's house. Today the Suarez family moved into Conga's old house. Nancy and Aracelio are very nice. They have two sons and their daughter is named Lourdes. I am sure Barbara and Elena will be happy to have more kids to play with. Today I see six to eight people taking over the bedrooms downstairs. There's a lady named Angela who seems to be in charge. Yeyo is rocking passively on the front porch, oblivious to the changes. I hold Barbara's hand and introduce myself.

"Hola, my name is Iluminada. I live in the back with my two daughters, Barbara and Elena.

You will see a lot of Barbara. She loves to be here with Yeyo. Welcome! I am sure you will like it here very much." She smiles at us and heads inside.

We've experienced so much uncertainty. There have been many changes since the revolution. I don't know what is staying or going. I keep to my routine. As I walk Barbara and Elena to their neighborhood school, I can hear chatter about our new neighbors. My girls receive free public education. Education is very important to me, and I will do everything under my power to help them graduate and choose good careers. All afternoon I sit and reflect. I am startled when I realize it is 3:00 p.m. Yeyo must be waiting for our daily game of canasta. It is our precious time together. His wits are not with him as much as before. I feel his mind is not thinking as clearly. Still, I have never met a more giving, gentle, and wise man. Angela approaches us and says, "Delio, your dinner is served." She rudely interrupts our game … and I was winning!

As I am getting Elena and Barbara ready for bed, I tell them that things might be different at the house. The new tenants need time to get to know us, and us them. The house will be full once again, just like in the old days. The difference is that it feels like an apartment house with tenants, not the family home it once was that was built with love and togetherness. I step outside onto my porch and see Nancy outside sitting on her balcony. We chat across the patios for a while. I am happy their family is here. I say a prayer for Yeyo and all of us.

NANCY & HER CHILDREN

THE PARK IN FRONT OF THE HOUSE

CARDECUYOTU

LOURDES & ARACELIO

LOURDES

Chapter 75

Three Hundred & Seven

We hitchhike regularly.

It is not only fun but free and reliable.

So many of us do it.

We meet fascinating people and enjoy every trip.

We use our thumbs to get to NYC, Storrs, and even for short trips around town.

I love going into Greenwich Village to buy fab leather vests, crocheted chokers, and beaded earrings.

We listen to 8-tracks on the trips.

The windows are down.

Folk music fills the air.

The words of Joan Baez, Bob Dylan, Neil Young, and Jackson Browne are regularly heard.

Most songs are anti-war.

They sound nothing like the music Lu would sing and dance to in Cuba.

Brian and I get back and forth between Bridgeport to UConn by hitching rides.

Brian failed out of Sacred Heart University, because his weekend trips to see me became Thursdays through Mondays.

He ended up never going to class.

It's Sunday, and we sit in my dorm room feeling creative.

I get my jeans out and cut them.

Then we insert a triangle in the front and back made from Brian's
jeans.
We have turned my bell bottoms into a skirt.
It is long and reaches my ankles. I wear it around campus.
No one has ever seen a jean skirt.
Everyone on campus stops me and asks me where I got it.
"I think we just invented something big, babe," Brian says.
"That's a gas," I say.

I'm in my dorm room.
All the girls are sitting in the hallway anxiously waiting for the
phone to ring.
Tears fill the corridors.
I wait for Brian's call.
Some girls are relieved, others devasted, all because of a number.
The higher the number, the better chance you have for not getting
drafted to Vietnam.
The line is ringing, and I am too scared to answer.
Lori, my roommate, says, "It's for you, Cuba."

His voice is shaky.
"Cuba, I love you."
"What number did you get?" I ask.
"9."
I drop to the floor.
"NO! NO! NO!"

I turn into a puddle.
"NO, BRIAN, NO!" I scream.
He tells me he loves me again.
"I have to go tell my sisters. Call you later," he says.

I struggle to get into my tiny bunk bed.
I pull the sheets over my head and cry for hours.

It is late.
The phone rings again.
"Hi, babe," Brian says cheerfully.
I cry loudly into the receiver.
"Babe," he says over my sobs.
"Babe! I have to tell you something."
"Lay it on me," I reply.
"My number is actually 307."

I am so relieved but so angry at the same time.
"I cannot believe you did that to me."
"Sorry, baby," he continues.
"Anyway, Dave is number 27. I think I am going to enlist and go
    with him. He's my best friend, I have to do it."
"I'm your best friend," I cry.
I plead with him to reconsider.
"Gotcha again!" he says.
"Shame on you!" I say.
Ever the joker, he apologizes.
He is safe for now.

I thank God and thank Papy for not letting Neny become a citizen
    when we did.
We are all U.S. citizens now, except Neny and Abuela.
Papy did not want Neny to become a citizen, so that he would be
    spared from the draft.

Abuela refused to get her citizenship.

She insists that because she was born in Tampa, Florida, she already is an American citizen.

But the hospital where she was born in 1897 was consumed by a fire, and all records were destroyed.

Her birth certificate lost.

"Four dead in Ohio," the radio informs us.

Four Kent State University students have been killed and many others injured on May 4, 1970. The Ohio National Guard fired shots into the crowd of Vietnam War protestors.

I hear the news while I am in the library at UConn.

I attend more rallies and marches.

I have become the protestor and rebel that I had always wanted to be.

My voice will be heard.

"STOP THE WAR!" I chant to myself as I fall asleep in my tiny bed.

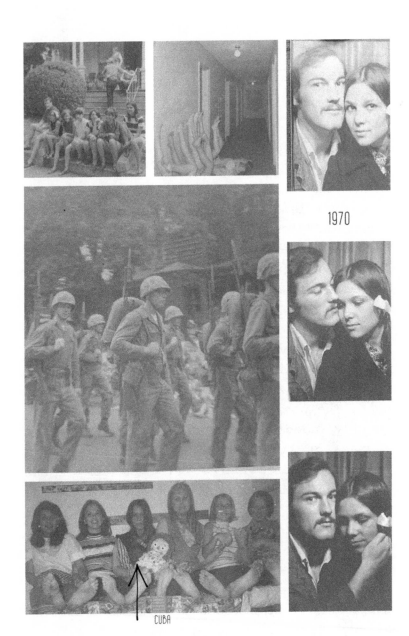

1970

CUBA

Chapter 76

Men

I have loved and I have lost. Luck has not been my friend in love. For me it has been a long, hard road. Barbara and Elena's father, Sergio, was a poor choice. Once he left us, I met José, who became the father of José and Ariel. His presence in our lives was even shorter. The men in my life have all gone. They deserted me and abandoned their children. In extremely difficult times, when we needed their companionship and support, they ran. My heart has many wounds and scars left by them. The passion we once felt for each other quickly faded when the music stopped, and the rawness of life settled. With children came responsibilities and a level of commitment that sent them running to the bars and to the arms of other lovers. I should have known that neither of them would make good partners. They couldn't even dance.

I continue to forge ahead, strong but alone. I have survived, but loneliness and despair have at times left me at the bottom, struggling to find the sunshine. My children are my driving force. The fairy tales I used to read to my girls remain frozen on the pages of the books. I hope they come alive for them. One day, I may find my prince, and I will make sure that he can cha-cha like a champion.

Conga & Lu

LU, BARBARA, & ELENA

Chapter 77

Red Roses and Paisley Dresses

Shortly after the massacre in Ohio, all the universities and colleges in the U.S. close.

I am sent home.

The semester is over early.

Back to work at Korvettes.

I also work on the weekends at the movie theater.

I wear a uniform and sell popcorn.

Brian and I watch many free movies when there are no customers.

I am engaged to Brian and decide to transfer to the University of Bridgeport.

I'm ready to start my life.

So far, all of the family weddings have been held in reception halls.

Papy borrowed five thousand dollars.

He wants to throw me a luxurious wedding at Hillandale Country Club.

His best friends are the priests from St. Mary's, where he works.

They will come to St Augustine Cathedral and officiate our wedding.

Yoly is my maid of honor.

Carmenchu, along with my high school friends Donna and Linda, are my beautiful bridesmaids.

Bibi is the flower girl, and little Roy is the ringbearer.
Brian's best buddy Dave is his best man.
Neny, Dave, and Billy complete the wedding party.
I borrow the family's *mantilla* (a veil) that has been passed down
    through Tensy and Carmenchu.
It is a new tradition we have started in the United States.

Brian and I do not want a big, extravagant wedding.
We had begged Papy to give us the money as a wedding present
    instead.
He refused.
We are broke, but Papy really wants this.
Brian and the boys wear tails.
He says he looks like a penguin; he does.
Mamy zips up my lace wedding gown.
I wear my long brown hair down and straight.
Mamy looks elegant as ever in her yellow skirt suit.
Her small buttery hat has gorgeous feathers.
She is always the most glamorous woman in the room.
Everyone in our wedding party carries just one long-stemmed red
    rose.
Each girl is so stunning, they don't need big bouquets.
My bridesmaids all wear paisley dresses.

It is a cold March afternoon.
I think it is one of the best days of Papy's life.
He is beaming like a light bulb.
My whole family and old Cuban friends come from Miami.
Gladis, Luis, Abuela Iraida, and Abuelo Pompeyo are here, too.
I wish Lu could be here.
My love for her is as strong as the last time I saw her.

The whole Giblin gang is here.
Spanish is flowing with the Silvas in their own space, but towards
the end everyone is mingling and having fun.
Turns out everyone speaks champagne.

Abuela did not make my cake, although she does make delicious
cakes.
Hers taste better than Zwerdlings, but after Tensy's wedding we all
were sick the next day.
We traced it back to the cake that had to travel so many hot miles
between Philly and New York City.
Abuela always says the secret to her delicious cake recipe is the
extra amount of eggs.
We found out eggs and high temperatures don't mix well.

Brian and I dance to "Lay Lady Lay."
That is our song.
Bob Dylan sings,

Stay, lady, stay, stay with your man awhile.
Why wait any longer for the world to begin.
You can have your cake and eat it too.
Why wait any longer for the one you love.
When he's standing in front of you.

We are happy the party is over.
Neither of us likes the formality of it.

We count the money we get from guests and relatives as
wedding gifts.
We book a honeymoon to the Bahamas!

Conga & Lu

We weren't sure if we would go to Europe or NYC.
It all depended on how much money we got.
We lucked out with the Bahamas!
I just have to convince my geology teacher to let me miss a week
of class.
I tell him I will bring him back some cool rocks and shells.
I wonder if the Bahamas will have the same beaches as Cuba.

I long to be warm and feel the Caribbean sun.

CUBA & BRIAN GIBLIN

Chapter 78

Asthma

My son José is very sick. His condition is worsening by the day. When he was born, he was diagnosed with asthma. He has lost much of his lung function. He has a chronic cough, and the doctors have told me his airway walls are thickening. I would give anything to make his life better. I would give him my every breath if I could.

He also has seizures, which are terrifying. He cannot walk or move on his own. My darling José is confined to one of many beds in the hospital, which is overflowing with patients. I feel fortunate that our healthcare is free. I would not be able to pay for all the time and treatments he receives. This time we have already been here for three months. His asthma is serious and getting worse. A young doctor informed me that José is at risk for respiratory failure, explaining it occurs when there is not enough oxygen traveling from your lungs to your blood. It pains me to no end to see him like this. His breathing is labored. He can barely open his eyes. I have been sitting here in this shared hospital room for months.

I try to sew but I cannot. All I can do is helplessly sit here alone and watch my boy. I memorize every line that shapes his face and every hair on his head. He has machines hooked up to him and a mask over his nose and mouth. My sister, and Elena's godmother Rita, have been taking care of my girls and Ariel, so they will not miss school. I try to stay strong, but as José sleeps, I weep. I weep for him, for my other children, and for all those who are ill.

Chapter 79

A Mother

I finish college in three years.

Brian paints and works to help support us.

I graduate with a major in Spanish and minors in education and French.

I get my first teaching job as a long-term substitute for a class that is filled with Portuguese children.

I love it.

On April 27, 1973, I become a mother.

My first-born is Cormac.

We live in Weston, Connecticut, and are caretakers for Weston Woods Studios.

The company produces audiotapes and short films that are based on famous children's books.

We clean their offices at night.

Brian is an office manager there during the day, so we get to stay rent free in one of the homes on the property.

Our house is small but perfect.

Two years later I have a daughter, Monet Iraida (named after my *abuela*).

Cormac's fourth birthday party is cowboy themed.

Everyone is dressed as cowboys, just like in Cuba.
His favorite gift is a holster with toy guns from Neny.

We tie-dye everything — clothes, curtains, bedspreads.
We make candles with paraffin.
The molds are cartons of milk and we use remnants of melted
    crayons for colors.
We learn all kinds of knots and make macramé jewelry and
    plant hangers.
We plant and eat bean sprouts, herbs, and tomatoes.
Everything grows in our rich Connecticut soil.
Incense burns on our coffee table, which Brian has made from
    stacked bricks and huge wooden spools.
The scent of patchouli permeates the air.
Large comfy floor pillows serve as our chairs.
The hot waterbed in our room keeps us warm.
Many bicycle tube patches serve as the bed's Band-Aids, so it won't
    spring a leak.
We are poor but happy.

The snow makes it hard for Brian to keep steady work as a
    house painter.
We survive on food stamps, which Brian wastes on treats
    and goodies.
Thank God for the WIC coupons.
With WIC coupons, we are able to get King Vitaman cereal, milk,
    eggs, bread, and other staples.
I don't like driving to East Main Street and knowing they must
    prick my children and test their blood to determine if we are
    eligible.

But they are slightly anemic, so we qualify.

We know Connecticut is not a place where we can continue to live.

We need to move somewhere with more opportunity.

The snow, which I once found magical and enchanting, I can no longer stand.

Our hands freeze, and our noses run.

We know we cannot stay.

INCENSE AND TIE-DYE
NENY GRADUATION GEORGETOWN MED SCHOOL
BRIAN, CORMAC, MONET, & CUBA
CORMAC
CORMAC & MONET
BRIAN, CUBA, MAMY, CORMAC & PAPY

Chapter 80

Heading South

After living in Connecticut for sixteen years, it is time to go.

It breaks my heart to leave Mamy and Papy, but I know we have no future here in Connecticut.

We have saved 900 dollars.

We pack our tie-dyed sheets and curtains, some of the wooden furniture, the picture frames Brian made, and all that we can fit into our VW bus.

We look at a map and determine we don't have enough money to make it to California.

So instead we head south to Florida.

It is so white we cannot see.

The snow falls in heaps and giant sheets.

A blizzard has rolled in to bid us a final goodbye.

Brian drives.

Cormac sits straddling the gearshift.

I have Monet on my lap and I am pregnant with our third child.

Brian starts driving down Black Rock Turnpike.

We don't get far before the roads are closed.

We have to turn back.

We pull up to my parents' house.

They think we have reconsidered and are not moving.

It snows for days, so we must stay until the roads are reopened.
As soon as the blizzard is over, we hit the road.
The cold is too much.
The opportunities limited.
We must leave Connecticut.
Half of my broken heart will stay here with Mamy and Papy.
With a heavy heart, but a longing to find our own piece of
happiness, we set off on our adventure.

We drive as far as our money takes us.
Joan Baez's beautiful voice singing "Gulf Winds" playing in our
cassette tape deck makes our journey enchanting.
We travel through many states in search of sunny skies and
warmer air.
We cross the state line and are finally in Florida.
This state is vast.
We drive down U.S. 41.
After countless bathroom breaks, both for the two little ones and
for me and my pregnant belly, we see the sign for Naples,
Florida.
We have never heard of it before.
Seems quiet.
Seems warm.
Gulf Winds — we have arrived!

Seems like the perfect place to raise our family.

BRIAN, MONET & CORMAC

↑CUBA IN CONNECTICUT AND FLORIDA↓

Chapter 81

Yeyo Is Gone

There is something happening at the house. I see people outside talking, crying. I am not sure what is happening but know that something feels wrong. I walk down the stairs. "What has happened?" I ask.

"Delio is gone," Angela says bluntly.

What? Delio has died? How could this be? I was just with him yesterday, playing cards. The lady of the house tells me it's no concern of mine. My heart aches. I begin to walk away, still processing the news. Another tenant grabs my arm and tells me Delio was brought to the hospital the night before. She said he had complained of a stomachache. When he arrived, doctors found he had a gastrointestinal blockage. He died early this morning. I thank her for telling me what happened.

I cannot believe that Delio is gone. He has meant so much to my family. My children felt like he was their grandfather. He was the only positive male figure in their lives. He helped me to provide for and care for my family. I always enjoyed my time spent with him. I struggle to find the words to tell my children their beloved Yeyo has passed. Barbara takes it the hardest. She screams, cries, then runs to the bedroom, slams the door, and locks herself in. It is a sad day. A very sad day.

I think of Conga and write her a letter. I struggle to find the right words to let her know that her dear grandfather has passed. As I walk to the mailbox, it begins to rain. Even God is crying.

DR. DELIO SILVA CASTRO

1896-1973

Chapter 82

Labor Pains

Our early days are rough.
No money, no friends, and no family.
I feel very alone without Papy and Mamy's love and support.
We are miles apart.
Their guidance, love, and wisdom are dearly missed.
We rent a duplex, like the one I lived in during my Miami exile.
On August 13, 1978, my daughter Sterling is born.

With Cormac, I had started labor pains at 3:00 a.m. but refused to
   go to the hospital.
Fourteen hours later with pains still, Brian, Mamy, and I went
   to Dairy Queen, and while standing in line waiting for our
   sundaes my water broke and I had to go straight from there
   to the hospital.
I was so embarrassed.

With Monet, Brian, who always liked fancy junk cars, had bought
   an old Mercedes.
After watching a midnight showing at the movies of *Tommy*, the
   rock opera, I got home with extreme pains.
I was already three weeks past my due date, so I was prepared with
   my overnight bag.
I guess Brian was not prepared yet.

Conga & Lu

The Mercedes ran out of gas on the Merritt parkway at 4:00 a.m.
I was considering the name Mercedes, since I was sure this baby
   would make her entrance in our car.
Brian had to hitchhike to a gas station. He made it back with some
   gas in a red can. Astonishingly, we made it to Bridgeport
   Hospital just in time.

When I was four months pregnant with Sterling, I went to several
   doctors to see if one could give me a break, since my pregnancy
   was already half over and we had no money.
We found an M.D. who agreed to help financially.
When Sterling's time came, Neny, Papy, Mamy, and Abuela were
   all visiting and crammed into our duplex.
Everyone came to the hospital.
Everyone except my doctor.
Several calls went unanswered to my obstetrician, but no one could
   find him.
It turned out he was moonlighting.
Another physician stepped in from the hall and was there to catch
   her head as it was coming out.
I don't remember who delivered her.
All I remember is a pair of blue eyes looking up at me with a smile
   saying, "It's a boy!"
It was not a boy.
It was a girl.

Monet loves her baby sister.
Sterling is her living doll.
Carmenchu has sent us a beautiful bassinet.
All the Silva babies use it.

That cradle traveled via Greyhound to whomever was having a
    baby, and Abuela always sewed the dressing.
Now it has made its way to Florida.

Sterling is a week old.
I place her in our bedroom in the bassinet.
She is sleeping.
I hear her cry, but I am making meatloaf.
I yell to Brian, "Get the baby!"
"Brian, Sterling is crying."
I must repeat myself five times.
The crying has stopped.
I hear a tiny voice coming into the kitchen, "I got her."
I look up and see two-year old Monet.
She is carrying our newborn baby Sterling by the neck across the
    house after taking her out of the bassinet herself.
I have to think quick and not panic so Monet won't drop her "doll."
"Thank you, Monet. Can I hold her now?"
My hands are still full of ground beef, but I grab the baby.
She is fine.
Hours pass, I place one of Monet's dolls in the bassinet and ask,
    "Monet, can you show me how you lifted baby Sterling out of
    the bassinet?"
I shouldn't have asked.
I am horrified.

It's a wonder Sterling survived.

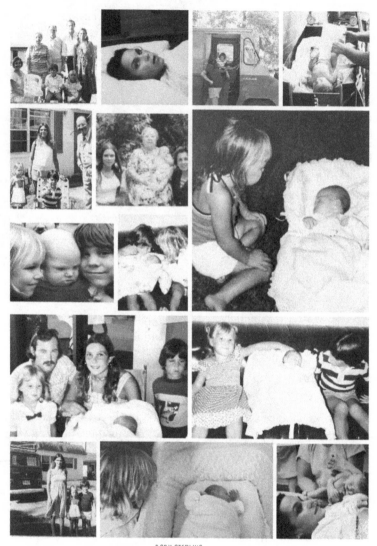

BABY STERLING

Chapter 83

True Colors

"Mama, Mama!" Barbara sobs uncontrollably as she scrambles up the stairs, skipping steps as she climbs. I can barely make out her words. Between sobs she says the people who live in CARDECUYOTU are making fun of her, calling her horrible names, and laughing at her in her face. She is devastated that our life has changed so drastically now that Yeyo is gone. The people that live here now have shown their true colors.

Those who in the beginning, when Yeyo was alive, accepted Barbara into the house are no longer kind. We are no longer welcome in the main house. One of the greatest injuries to a mother's heart happens when she feels her children are being mistreated. I cry for my children. Their pure, innocent hearts cannot understand the reasons these people are treating them badly. Are they jealous? Is it because we are black? I don't really know.

All doors and windows to the house are shut. They make us take the back way into our home above the garage. I feel that they think we are a living threat. The new lady of the house has moved in many relatives. She feels powerful, and I can tell she is the one in command. She is selling all of the beautiful things that were inside the house. I see them remove the lovely furnishings, artwork, and most of the contents of the home and load them into many vehicles on the street. We do not feel comfortable in our little home.

I hear a loud knock at the door. I open it to find Angela, who lives in the main house. "You are not welcome here. Pack your things and get your family out. Either leave now or I will notify officials and I will see you in court." Eviction? How could she be so heartless? Sending a single mother with four small children, one bedridden, into the streets? I hug Elena, Barbara, Ariel, and José tight and watch them sleep.

A few days later there is another knock. I peer out of the curtains and see a few policemen outside. My kids are scared and crying. Two-year-old Ariel is clinging to my leg. I tell Barbara to run and get Rita. I am escorted out and driven to the courtroom. My palms are sweaty and I feel drops of cold sweat dripping down my back. Our future depends on the court's ruling — eviction or not? I still cannot believe that Angela is trying to throw us out of our home. Even Yeyo had told me once, "That woman doesn't understand anything." I must do all that I can to protect my family. The judge does not take long to reach his decision. We win! For now. We can continue to live in CARDECUYOTU.

So much has changed since that young girl from Matanzas first entered this loving home that Cuban spring day in 1956, looking up at the heavens with optimism and joy.

ELENA AND FRIEND

Chapter 84

The Storm

The wind continues to batter our small apartment. Outside all I see is white. The rain is coming down in sheets, not drops. I am huddled in the living room with my babies. We filled the bathtub with water. The lights flicker, then a loud boom, now darkness. The electricity is gone.

Barbara, Elena, Ariel, and José all stay close on the sofa. We have been through many storms, but this one is fierce and violent. I don't know how much longer we can take it. I hear more smashing and startling noises. We shiver as branches crack and windows break.

"Come closer," I say to Elena. In the candlelight, I begin to tell them a story about a fisherman. A loud thud stops me mid-sentence. I know our home is in danger. The water reservoir that the new tenants of CARDECUYOTU installed on our roof comes crashing into our living room. Rain comes rushing in. I scramble to get all of us to the kitchen. I struggle to get some pillows for José and make a bed for him on the floor. He is very weak. Ariel and the girls are crying. We are alone.

We must ride out this storm together. I will stay strong and brave for them. We are quarantined in our kitchen for hours while the storm savagely rips apart our home. After hours I can tell the rain is lightening, and the wind no longer sounds like a freight train. I get up to look out the window, which has been shattered. Devastation.

The giant mamey tree is uprooted and thrown, covering the entire back yard. Cracked branches are scattered everywhere. I open the front door to find the trunk has dislodged our spiral staircase. The stairs are completely unusable, split in half. We have no way to get down. We are trapped. We sit in terror for hours. Day turns to night, night becomes dawn. Finally, I hear people below. The police are here. They help us all safely down.

We can no longer live in our home. With tears in my eyes, I say goodbye to CARDECUYOTU. I take the few belongings we have that were not destroyed by the storm and the memories I have in my heart. I say farewell to the place where I have lived and worked for over twenty-five years. Government officials bring us to a homeless shelter. There are many others who, like us, have no place to live. I pray our time here will be short.

Chapter 85

Kool-Aid and Potatoes

We live off Kool-Aid and baked potatoes.

We borrow $5,000 from my parents to buy a piece of land.

Brian paints houses.

Construction is booming in southwest Florida.

He always provides for us.

We have enough for a deposit to start building a small house on land in Naples, Florida.

We buy a 1.25-acre lot in Golden Gate Estates.

There are cabbage palms, cypress trees, and pines as far as the eye can see.

Brian climbed the highest Sabal Palm so that he could to get a good view of our new land.

He made it up but came down with his hands and thighs full of splinters.

I love the heat and nature; the well water not so much.

The beaches are beautiful, but still Cuba's shores remain unrivaled.

We have struggled, yet we have succeeded.

We are blessed.

Brian has become a firefighter.

Even on his off days, if we see a brush fire, we have to go track it down.

I am now the one ironing his uniform and spraying the starch to make sure it is perfect, just like Lu had done for me.

I think of her often.

Cormac is in kindergarten.

He rides the bus.

It is 3:00 p.m., and I wait at the bus stop on Indiana Avenue.

The bus comes and some children get off, but there is no Cormac.

I run home pushing Sterling in her stroller, with Monet trying to
keep up.

I frantically call the school.

No answer.

Brian is at work at the fire station.

His shifts are twenty-four hours on and forty-eight off.

Today he is on.

I take a taxi to the school.

I find a custodian.

I explain my boy is missing.

He makes some calls.

It has been hours.

Darkness is approaching.

I am losing my mind.

Where could he be?

Finally, we have word that he has been located.

He was found sitting on the bus by himself in the dark garage, very
calm, cool, and collected.

He was so small and the seats so high, the driver never saw him.

It turns out they changed the bus numbers that day and he got on
the wrong bus.

The bus he was on never went to our stop.

I run to him and hug him tightly.

"Why did you just sit there for so long?" I ask.

Cormac answers, "You said never get off the bus if you do not see
your stop. I never saw my stop."

I hug him tightly.

"I love you," I tell him.

I think I have my first gray hairs.

We send Cormac and Monet to Bridgeport to spend the summer
with Mamy and Papy.

I pin a note to Cormac's chest saying, "My Name is Cormac Giblin.
I am traveling to Bridgeport, Connecticut. If I am lost, please
call Cuba Giblin at 813-455-3205."

I give them kisses and tell Cormac to take care of his sister.

I imagine how hard it must have been for Mamy and Papy to send
Neny and I alone to Miami so long ago.

I put them on the plane and pray they find Papy and Mamy waiting
for them on the other side when they land.

The living room in Mamy and Papy's home in Bridgeport is
converted into one big "playroom" for the children.

There are life-sized playhouses made out of old refrigerator boxes
and wallpaper.

Old shelves are laid on the ground. They are now highways for
matchbox cars.

Baby dolls sit in circles having permanent tea parties.

Cups tied together with strings make telephones.

Entire action figure sets, Army men, and Barbie dolls are always
positioned ready for play.

It is a child's paradise.

But the best part is Mamy and Papy are right there sitting on
the floor in the middle of it all, playing with their grandchildren.

Neny lives in California.

After graduating from medical school, he did his residency in California and knew he would stay there.

He loves it.

Papy has had a terrible health scare.

He endured a major heart attack walking the snowy streets of Bridgeport coming home from work.

He was operated by the best heart surgeon, Dr. Debakey, in Houston, Texas.

Being a doctor, Neny was able to facilitate this.

I had to suffer silently in Florida as he had his open heart and valve put in.

It was a major surgery.

When he got back to Bridgeport, Papy learned he had contracted hepatitis from a blood transfusion during surgery.

After we almost lost him, he pulled through.

Abuela, who still always seemed to know who needed her at what moment, took a Greyhound bus and spent four months nursing Papy back to health, while Mamy went back to work.

Abuela was living in Philadelphia with Carmenchu at the time.

Papy could not return to work.

I think Papy's heart broke when we left.

Mamy and Papy decide to move again.

They choose Florida.

They live for their grandchildren.

It's not CARDECUYOTU, but they buy the lot right next to us, and
they build their new home.
We have a little dirt path through the woods that leads from our
house to theirs.
That path sees more traffic than I-75.
They call it *La Sierra*.
Papy nails a sign to the cypress tree.
It reads "*Los Quiticos*" (the little ones) with an arrow pointing to
our house next door.
They turn their third bedroom into an "estudio" for Papy's desk,
bookshelves, diplomas, and awards.
There's a little stand in the room for Mamy's typewriter, too.
There must be hundreds of books on the shelves.
Every Friday is "payday" for *Los Quiticos*.
Papy would sit behind his desk and hand out small manila
envelopes with each of their grandchild's names on them with
a few dollars allowance enclosed in each.

I love that my parents tell my children stories of Cuba.
We speak Spanish often.
They pick it up quickly — all but Brian, who still refuses to learn,
and my youngest, Sterling, who says, "Don't talk like that,"
when we have conversations in Spanish.

We are together. Life is good.

STERLING, CUBA, MONET

MONET & CORMAC

CORMAC, STERLING, & MONET

CORMAC, MONET, CUBY, NENY

CORMAC, MAMY, MONET

CITY OF NAPLES FIRE DEPT

Chapter 86

The Shelter

The smells of urine, vomit, and spit will forever remain with me. I'm thankful to be here yet saddened by the circumstances I find family in. Days are turning into weeks, weeks are turning into months, months are turning into years. We accommodate as best we can. The one pillow allotted to each of us we give to José. When propped up, his labored breathing eases. I go with him to the hospital when it is necessary, leaving my children in the care of trusted friends. Barbara and Elena are stoic. They do not complain. They go to school and continue to live their lives as normally as possible. There's a small courtyard in back of our shelter where they can play with the other children living here. Ariel is so young he does not understand where he is. José is too sick to realize. I have to be creative to hold my small family together. I read them children's books. We play board games. We listen to and sing songs. We play hopscotch and jump rope outside. People, for the most part, are kind and caring. We have a roof above our heads and three hot meals a day. The shelter is safe. When we lose electricity, which happens quite often, or a raging Cuban storm passes, my children become frightful once again. They still have nightmares about the terrible storm that brought us here. I reassure them we are safe. However, it is very crowded. As mothers and children come and go, we are able to change to better quarters — near a window, closer to a fan, not far from toilets, etc. A community feeling permeates the shelter. The heartache and suffering of all those we meet here is unforgettable, but I remain grateful.

Chapter 87

Shark Teeth and Swim Meets

Cormac pretends he is a judge in Papy's study.

Monet is at swim practice.

Sterling is always outside with the animals.

We have goats, chickens, a pig, a tortoise, cats, dogs, hamsters, fish, snakes, hermit crabs, geckos, mice, and birds.

It's like our own *finca*.

Brian surprised me by getting a pony.

He had Sterling ride it into the kitchen.

I now know how Mamy felt when I would surprise her with new pets in Cuba.

We named him Chachi.

Papy would walk Chachi down the street every day to meet the kids at the bus stop.

One day after he put Cormac on Chachi's saddle, the pony took off at a full gallop towards home, leaving Papy and Monet standing there helpless.

One and a half miles later, Chachi had galloped all the way down the street and right into his stable behind our house.

I asked Cormac how he directed the pony home so well.

He told us he didn't even have a hold of the reins.

All he did was grab on for dear life.

I'm happy Chachi was not as wild as Tormenta!

The pony knew exactly where to go.

Conga & Lu

We have so many animals and nature abounds.
Cormac once found a baby alligator alone by the canal and he
     brought it home.
The kids were sad that we could not keep him.

Sometimes nature gets too close.
We have found pygmy rattlesnakes in our closets and scorpions
     in our T-shirts.
There have been ticks on us, too.
What an ordeal it was to try to burn a fat one full of blood off of
     Monet's ear.
I once caught Sterling with a palmetto bug dangling from her
     mouth.

We are always on outdoor adventures.
From sandbars to sharks' teeth, swim meets to space shuttles,
     snorkeling to Shark Valley, we see it all.
We visit Disney World, Epcot, and Busch Gardens.
We are always going somewhere.
We experience all of Florida.
From Pensacola to Key West.

Exploring off the beaten path is what we love.
Whether it is abandoned oyster canning factories in Apalachicola
     or canoeing to Mud Bay in the Ten Thousand Islands, we are
     always ready for an adventure.
Naples is the perfect spot for us.
Brian is always taking us to new places.
We pick oranges down the road.
We also go mango hunting.
They are everyone's favorite.

I must ration them or huge fights break out.
It is easy to see who has tried to sneak them.
Cormac and Sterling are covered in bumpy red rashes as soon as
the juice touches their faces, but they cannot resist.

We stroll to the canal.
The kids like to pick the cattails and watch them explode when
they bloom.
There are also alligators in there.
I tell the kids to stay out, but I know they dare each other to swim
across. They try to hide their wet clothes outside, but I know
better.
We take hose baths and play in sprinklers in the yard.
We bike and skate and Slip N' Slide.

We spend hours at the beach finding starfish, coquinas, sea glass,
and sand fleas.
We spot stingrays gliding through the hot water.
One sizzling summer Sunday at Wiggins Pass, Papy forgot to do
the stingray shufflele and stepped on one.
It was another trip to the emergency room.
Cormac and Brian are not expert fishermen, but they do try.
The pier and the bridges are usually good spots, but it's mostly
catfish on their hooks.
While they fish, the girls collect shells and perfect their drip
sandcastle techniques.

We don't belong to a yacht club like Miramar, but we do sneak into
the Naples Beach Club hotel.
Brian and I order drinks, and the kids use the pool and beach all
day long.

The Beach Club has a diving board and the kids take turns doing
    cannonballs as tourists try to stay dry.

It's not the *finca*, but we get lost camping in the Everglades.
We go boating in the Gulf.
We go tubing, wake boarding, and hydro-sliding.
We let the slow current off of Keewaydin Island take us for rides
    to the end of the inlet.
We follow dolphins, watch manatees, and explore vacant houses.
As Brian captains the boat, I yell to him, "Decrease the speed on
    the turns."
He still likes to drive fast.
Motorcycles, cars, boats — it doesn't matter.
Without fail, on every outing, we get stuck in the deep, black mud.
No one wants to jump off and push.
The sand is squishy, and seaweed creeps in between toes.
Our boat is often seen on a sandbar.

Friends always fill our home.
Everyone loves the Giblin House.
The kids ride their ATCs and ATVs through the woods.
They make forts with palm frond roofs and pine needle flooring.

There is no place I'd rather be.

Chapter 88

A New Home

The government helped us get an apartment
sooner than others, since José's medical
condition is so severe. We now have a nice
apartment in our old neighborhood, La Víbora,
on the second floor of a building just blocks
from CARDECUYOTU. We have two bedrooms, a
living room, dining room, bathroom, and a
balcony. I spend much time, when I am not in
the hospital, outside on the balcony. It is hot
inside and the fresh air does my body good.
I like to watch the stories of the neighborhood
unfold before my eyes as I sit and watch.

I have some pains in my legs, but they
come and go. Life is hard. We have enough,
but nothing is wasted or taken for granted. We
must ration our food. I must get creative with
birthday presents. Still, we are together, and
I am grateful.

NEW APARTMENT IN LA VIBORA

Chapter 89

Soup or Salad

Neny is here visiting us.

He comes every year.

He is an internist in Fountain Valley, California.

The kids love when he visits.

We go roller-skating, to the drive-in, and to the movies.

They pile into our Fiat and are off to the toy store, Playland, in the Coastland Center mall.

He lets them choose anything they want.

Sterling chooses a stuffed animal, Monet a beautiful doll for her collection, and Cormac a whole assortment of G.I. Joe men.

They stop to play some *Pitfall* and *Pac-Man* at the Gold Mine arcade.

Cormac sits eating the last spoonful of an entire jar of marshmallow fluff.

Monet is emptying the last of the Life cereal, which she has devoured in one sitting.

I catch Sterling sneaking into the refrigerator with half of a raw hot dog in her mouth.

"Let's go out to eat!" Neny says.

"I think they're hungry," I say.

I remove the half hot dog from Sterling's mouth and put it in our dog Scruffy's bowl.

We got Scruffy from the Humane Society.
She is the protector of the house.

We love eating at Fujiyama's Japanese Steak house when Neny
visits.
It is a special treat.
Monet and Sterling emerge from Mamy's closet, each with a pair
of her highest *tacones*.
They have doused themselves in *Agustin Reyes' Agua de Violetas*, too.
They have overdone it, and the floral smell is overpowering.
"Ready!" they reply.

Neny teaches us to make bras and bows from our cloth napkins.
He tells us Pepito jokes, and before we know it, it is time to order.
Mamy orders "crap."
We laugh as she repeats herself again and again.
The waitress is puzzled.
"Crab," I say to the waitress. "Do you have crab?"
Next she asks Papy, "Will you have soup or salad?"
"Yes," he says.
He wonders what makes the salad "super."
My children chuckle again.
Papy can't wait for his "super salad" to arrive.
They have learned so much English, but there are still times when
their Cuban roots are exposed.
We laugh as the chef lights the table on fire and throws shrimp
into Brian's pocket.
We ask the waitress to snap a photo.
Cormac and Neny make obnoxious faces while Mamy quickly
removes her glasses and flashes her movie-star pose.

The bill arrives.
Papa reaches for it, and he looks surprised.
"Fujiyama, *no me llama*," he says. Fujiyama, don't call me.
It is very expensive.

It must've been the crap ... or maybe the super salad.

FUJIYAMA

NENY, MAMY, STERLING, ALI, BRIAN, CORMAC, MONET, GABY, KATHY & PAPY

Chapter 90

Popeye, Smurfette, and a Kitty Cat

We celebrate often.

Halloween is one of our favorite days.

Mamy and Papy are always our first trick-or-treaters.

Papy always looks through the candy bowl and picks out the Milky Ways.

Mamy decorates with the giant *bruja* (witch) that would scare all the children.

Cormac and Monet are too big for the felt kitty cat costumes that our neighbor made in Connecticut.

They wore them until the pants became shorts.

Sterling will be the kitty cat this year.

She still fits.

Monet chooses Smurfette.

I tell her we don't need to buy one.

"I will make it."

I am not a great seamstress.

I make the white hat and attach long yellow yarn strands.

A light white sundress will do.

We cover her in blue paint.

Even I think she looks ridiculous, but it is too late to get another one.

Cormac has insisted he wants a store-bought costume this year.
We find a plastic Popeye costume and mask at Kmart.
We head out.
We are on the third house, and Cormac is sweating profusely.
No air can enter the suit, and heat builds up inside the plastic.
He has created his own sauna.
He is dripping and red.
We keep walking.
Onto the fifth house, his pants split open and the sleeves rip.
Now Popeye's really showing his muscles.
Monet is leaking blue everywhere.
Her white dress looks tie-dyed with blue paint splattered all over.
The paint mixes with sweat and is getting into her eyes.
Sterling is hanging on my leg.
She does not want to walk anymore.
No amount of candy is worth this torture.

We decide next year we will trick-or-treat at the mall.

CORMAC, STERLING & MONET

SMURFETTE, MAMY, & A KITTY CAT

PAPY & MAMY

Chapter 91

Mother Goose

I am a teacher.
I know this is what I was meant to do.
The experiences I had as a refugee help guide my lessons.
I see hope and courage in my students.

Brian is now a battalion chief at the fire station.
During the nights he works, the kids have a rotation of who gets
    to sleep in my big bed.
We have contests to see who falls asleep first.

We also own Giblin Painting.
Only having one telephone line, we would have to answer, "Giblin
    Painting, how can we help you?" every time we answered the
    phone.
Brian has all of us sanding, priming, and sweating in the garage
    or out in our front yard.

Fridays are the best.
We love when Brian gets paid.
He sings, "We're in the money," and hundred-dollar bills line our
    bedroom mirror.
Then we go out to happy hour to celebrate with kids in tow.
Sometimes Sterling would even nap under the table.
She can sleep anywhere!

Mamy and Papy help with getting the kids to where they need
to go.
Papy drives a huge maroon Plymouth Fury.
He races into Golden Gate Elementary.
All the teachers know to guard the kids and move the car line back
when they see him approach.
He often neglects to slow down and pops up on the curb.
The safety patrol opens the door, and everyone can hear the *"Pete's
Dragon"* audio book blaring from the cassette player.

Not having much money, I have to find free camps for my kids in
the summer.
Some are great, like cooking, making jams shorts, and rocket
building.
Some are awful, like the summer they spent learning about sewage
at water treatment plants and how they make potable water
for irrigation.

School comes easily for all three of my children.
I read to them every night.
An anthology of Mother Goose nursery rhymes is always their
first choice.
I cut up photos of each of them and place them on different pages.
They get so excited to see themselves in the book with the other
characters.

Another of my children's favorite stories *is Peter Pan.*
Papy loves to tell it to them.
"Let me tell you the story of Peter Pan," says Papy.
They have heard the tale before, but they all sit excitedly for the
way Papy tells stories.

He tells of Peter's adventures.

He explains how there are only children in Neverland and tells of the Lost Boys' fun.

"Did you know your mother was a lost boy?"

Their eyes open wide.

"Really, Papa?" asks Sterling.

"Yes, she was part of a special operation called *Operacíon Pedro Pan*. Thousands and thousands of children escaped Castro's Cuba alone, hoping to return to their parents soon. Your mother was one of them. Tata and I sent her and Uncle Neny on an airplane filled with only children on a secret mission to Miami. She couldn't even tell her grandparents she was leaving! Her life, like Peter Pan's, has been filled with adventures ever since."

As they grew older, Monet likes to read Dickens.

All I can get Cormac to read is *Mad Magazine*.

At two or three, Sterling told me, "Teach me how to read. I don't want to wait for someone to read me a story. I want to read when I want to read."

My children are all gifted students.

I leave them a word of the day on the kitchen table each day during the summer. I really think it helps build their vocabulary.

One of my favorite games when I first arrived from Cuba was to open the dictionary and quiz myself and others on English words.

I'm convinced that is how I learned English so quickly.

MONET & CORMAC

STERLING

HANDMADE JAMS ↑

CUBA'S CLASSROOM

Chapter 92

A Changed Cuba

My country has changed. The biggest holiday is July 26th. All of us are obligated to go hear Fidel speak in Havana. The bus picks us up in the morning and brings us into the city. Fidel's speeches always stir up the crowd. He is a gifted speaker.

The conditions here are extreme. Many who years ago were very excited about the revolution and Fidel's promises have become jaded. We lose our electricity almost daily. Materials are hard to come by, but we press on. We are Cubans. We learn to adapt and to improvise. We have become masters at repurposing things and bringing new life to objects that no longer function. Everything can always be used for something. It just takes a little imagination and ingenuity.

Barbara and I head to the store to pick up the two cans of juice we are allotted. We bring them to the table where the *Judicio Popular* sits. The *Judicio Popular* is a jury that decides if we get the items or not. They ask us what we need them for. I tell them we

are out and my children would enjoy drinking
their juice in the mornings. The Jury decides
we will not be permitted to leave with the
juice today. They tell me to come back next
week. We leave empty-handed but hopeful that
next week we will have better luck.

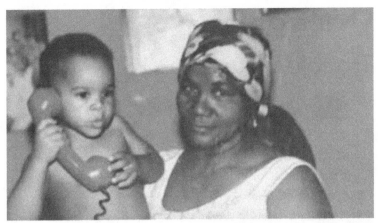

ILUMINADA & WILLIAM

PLAZA DE LA REVOLUCIÓN

Chapter 93

Troublemakers

Naples, Florida, is a small town.

There is not much for kids to do.

Especially in the '80s.

Sometimes, when left to their own devices, they get into trouble.

Brian and I left the kids for a weekend with 100 dollars for food and emergencies.

We came back to a bare pantry and hungry kids, but a new Nintendo Power Pad.

One boring summer day Monet and Sterling decided to walk to the mall.

It is a good six-mile trek from our house in Golden Gate Estates to the Coastland Center.

They hadn't told me they were going.

I received a collect call from them from a pay phone asking me to come pick them up.

Hot and exhausted, they had not realized they didn't bring any money, so they couldn't even get a drink at the food court.

They also never thought ahead about having to walk all the way home.

I'm surprised they didn't have heat stroke.

Monet and Sterling are playing in Papy's study.

They're supposed to be doing chores.

They discover how fun it is to open the sofa bed, have Sterling lay
    in it, then fold the bed up with Sterling hiding inside.
They call me to the room to show me.
My reaction is not what they expected.
"Don't ever do that again!" I say. "It's dangerous. You could
    suffocate."
I think their game is over.
I go back outside to weed.

Unbeknownst to me, they continue the game.
This time Monet tells Sterling that she wants a turn to be rolled
    into the bed.
Monet gets in and Sterling makes the couch up, pillows and all.
She sits on the couch.
I go and check to see if they are organizing the closet.
I see the couch perfectly made up and Sterling reading.
"All done," she says.
I go back outside.

Sterling is too little to pull the bed up.
Monet is freaking out inside the mattress sandwich.
It is getting hot.
"Get someone!!!" Monet's muffled voice screams.
Sterling doesn't want to get me, for fear they will be punished for
    not listening.
With one last heroic pull, and the strength of ten firemen, little
    Sterling is able to open the bed.
Monet is freed and gasps for air.
Cormac runs out the door to find me.
He was always sure to report any incidents.
I was happy to hand over the weeding to the girls.

Conga & Lu

Mamy and Papy have gone to California to spend Christmas with Neny, his wife Kathy, and my nieces Alessandra and Gabriella.

We decide to bring over a Christmas tree and set it up at Mamy and Papy's house.

We will decorate their home for the holiday so they can celebrate with us when they return from Fountain Valley.

As we enter the driveway, we see it is full of cars.

We see several teens going in.

As soon as we open the door, we hear Guns N' Roses blaring.

Teenagers are everywhere.

They see us and start to scatter.

The music stops.

Well, needless to say the party is over.

I am sure Cormac will be sanding louvres until his fingers bleed all weekend.

Brian and I decide to sell our house and build a new one.

It will be TWO STORIES, and everyone is most excited about having a POOL.

However, we do not have money for land or a down payment until we sell the home we are living in.

We sell our house and move in with Mamy and Papy while we build our new house.

It is a few miles away, a bit closer to town, and Brian has decided to build it himself.

All the firemen have side jobs.

As an owner-builder, we have our friends do the plumbing, the roofing, the framing ... anything.

However, this adds significant time to the building process.

What started out as a few months of all seven of us living in Mamy and Papy's house turned into a year and a half.

Brian and I sleep in the guest bedroom.

Every night the girls sleep on the pull-out couch in Papy's Study.

Mamy pulls out Cormac's pin pan pun, the cot he would sleep in and set it up in the living room.

It is cramped, but we make so many great memories.

Like our years in Miami, it is the tough times when the family pulls together that I end up loving the most.

I will be forever grateful to my parents, who have been here for me always.

Conga & Lu

CALIFORNIA CHRISTMAS

Chapter 94

CDR

In every neighborhood, Revolution! This is the purpose of the Committees for the Defense of the Revolution, or CDR. They are known as the "eyes and ears of the Revolution."

There is a committee in every neighborhood that is responsible for knowing everything about everybody on each block. The CDR was formed in 1960 after a bomb went off while Fidel was giving a speech in front of what used to be the presidential palace. The CDR keeps records of all who come and go, what activities we are involved in, and with whom we meet. We are always being watched.

Our block president, Juan Manuel, collects and reports all the information about every citizen in on our street. Dulce is a member of the CDR. She handles the ideology and makes sure we all receive political material. She distributes pamphlets throughout the neighborhood that inform us of many successes of the Revolution. I read today on the notice that our literacy rates are very high. Literacy is taken very seriously in Cuba.

Conga & Lu

Today I go to the CDR with my daughters. Barbara will receive a new pair of shoes. The woman takes Barbara's paper, then disappears behind a wall for several minutes. She reappears, pumps in hand. She hands Barbara some black *tacones*. No box, no bag, just the shoes. High heels are given to all women who work in office jobs. Barbara also receives a pair of black stockings. She is very excited to begin her job.

BARBARA

Chapter 95

Accidents Happen

We have been through our share of accidents and close calls.
I wish Neny lived closer.
We could use a good doctor around.

Monet was wearing her new Polly Flinders dress and looking
    beautiful on her seventh birthday.
Brian was giving the girls pony rides on the horse.
No one must have noticed the steaming horse poop patties that
    Chachi had left by the fence.
Monet was sprinting playing a game, looking for a hidden $10 bill.
She slid through the manure and right into the huge cactus in our
    front yard.
She was pierced all over her body.
It took hours to get out the needles.

While we were building our second home in Naples, the kids were
    riding an ATC on the dirt road behind the house.
"Mom, hurry!!!" Monet cries as she runs through the trees to find me.
I drop the broom and run to the neighbors to call 911.
The ambulance takes them to the emergency room.
All is OK — Sterling and Cormac are fine.
It was a bloody wreck, but no broken bones or stitches.
Leaving the hospital, Cormac and Sterling are already fighting
    with each other.

"Stop, guys."

Monet is the constant moderator between them.

At the Collier County Fair, while we were ordering our elephant ears, Sterling went around the back of the booth.

She found a cute dachshund.

She leaned in to pet it, and it took a chunk out of her cheek.

She needed six stitches on her face.

Cormac got a set of lawn darts for his birthday.

He was throwing them, and Monet was marking how far he had tossed them.

After checking the last landing spot, Monet started to dance where he was throwing.

"Move!" Cormac shouted.

Monet continued to dance and had added cartwheels to her routine.

"Move," he said again.

Monet wasn't going anywhere; she was twirling like a ballerina.

Cormac took the blue dart and hurled it.

Monet spun around, and as soon as she faced us, she saw the dart and screamed.

The dart pierced her foot next to her big toe.

Cormac turned white.

I ran for Brian.

Monet had Rowena, a foreign swimmer from England, coming to spend ten days with us.

You would have thought the queen herself was coming the way Mamy was cleaning.

Finally, her last room to ready up was Papy's study.

She climbed onto a chair to get the curtains down.

Conga & Lu

Mamy slipped, fell, and braced herself with her arms.
She ended up with casts on each arm and two broken wrists.
She couldn't do anything.
Poor Cormac had to make his own iced tea.

Mamy picks Sterling up from Naples High.
One day she entered the bus loop instead of the car line, just as a
    bus was pulling out.
No injuries … but Sterling was so humiliated.
The entire student body saw her grandma hit the school bus.

Cormac thinks he is either the Karate Kid or Hulk Hogan.
I'm not sure which.
He wrestled our neighbor Clayton and ended up with a broken leg.
Cormac also went knee-boarding with his friends on senior skip
    day and busted his lip.
We held our breath waiting for him to arrive at Barron Collier
    High School.
He was almost unrecognizable at his graduation with his busted
    lip and twenty-three stitches, covered in paint.
He wanted to drive himself.
The only car available was Brian's painting van.
He took a turn too fast and ending up receiving his diploma while
    white paint was still drying on his pants.

At least he made it in time.

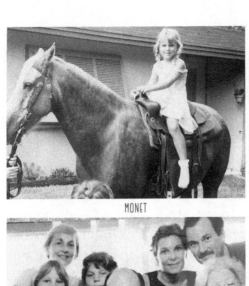

MONET

CORMAC, CUBA, BRIAN, STERLING & MONET

MAMY, CUBA, BRIAN, MONET, CORMAC, STERLING, PAPY & ABUELA

CORMAC

371

Chapter 96

Goodbye, José

José has left us. I have no words. It is the single worst day of my life. I must remain strong for my children, but the pain brings me to my knees. I pray he is in a better place, free of pain and suffering. His kind heart and gentle spirit will always be a part of me. He remains with me always.

Chapter 97

Cuba Vivian Fabiola de Fatima Pérez Silva Amargos Herrera Bonachea Castro Herrada Herrera Palmero Céspedes Prieto Núñez Rivadeneira

Abuela Cuba comes to visit.
She stays for one month every year.
She travels by herself, lives by herself, and is as strong as ever.
And she still makes the best *croquetas* I have ever tasted in my life.

All the Silvas reunite for special occasions.
Our large Cuban family is still very close.
We have family reunions often.
At least every ten years, the entire Silva family gets together.
We take over cruise ships in our matching shirts, and the children
    are free to explore and get to know all their cousins.
For Abuela's 80th and 90th birthdays, we met in Philadelphia.
She has twelve grandchildren.
Nine of us were born in Cuba and three were born in the United
    States during our Cuban exile — Beatriz, Jorge, and Cuba-Elena.

As a child in Cuba, I remember the lavish parties at
    CARDECUYOTU.

Conga & Lu

One of Abuela's passions was entertaining and hosting elegant
affairs.
The excitement was felt by all during the days of preparation.
Now, years later, I still feel the spark she emanates.
When a party is mentioned, she is the first one to start planning
the menu and charting lists of things to do.
Even at 100 years old, her excitement is contagious, and I love to
watch it grow.
She would say, "The importance is that the food is cooked and
served, and the guests who are in attendance. The rest takes
care of itself."

We also got together for Abuela's 100th birthday celebration.
She has lived an amazing life across three centuries.
I cannot begin to explain the love, the strength, and the courage
she has for her family.
Abuela died at the age of 103.
She will always be the hero of our family.
I know she is proud of all that we have accomplished together.

We celebrate birthdays in a big way.
Brian, Sterling, and my granddaughter Keagan all have birthdays
on August 13th.
They happen to share their birthday with Fidel Castro.
I used to wish Fidel had never been born, but without his birth
I would not have any of them in my life.

So many presidents have come and gone.
Eisenhower, Kennedy, Johnson, Nixon, Ford, Carter, Reagan, Bush,
Clinton, another Bush, and Obama have led our country.
Yet the Castros are still in command of the small island nation.

Even the Iron Curtain has fallen.

The Berlin Wall was built and came tumbling down, yet communism still controls Cuba.

Many Silvas have settled in Florida.

I guess Cuba has an invisible pull on the family.

It draws us near.

We are as close as we can be to our homeland.

Mamy, Papy, Uncle René, Aunt Yolanda, Olga, Tony, Tonito, Renecito and his wife Elena, and Chuchin and his wife Marcia have all joined us.

Sadly, Abuela Iraida and Abuelo Pompeyo have passed on.

I will carry the quiet dignity Abuelo Pompeyo always showed.

Abuela Iraida's passion for nature and all living things I carry in my heart.

Together they were a beautiful force that helped shape my young life.

My cousin Yoly has also passed. She died at age 39 from complications from a surgery.

I hope her sons Michael and Mark inherit her undeniable zest for life, laughter, and humor.

She dedicated her life to educating immigrant students in Detroit, Michigan. I carry a place in my heart for her.

Aunt Gladis still lives in Miami with her husband Luis and their children Luis Juan and Ana Maria.

They keep the candles by the statue of San Lazaro burning brightly daily.

I am a teacher.

I have taught every grade from preschool to adult education in Collier County.

I have my dream job of teaching those who are learning English as their second language, as I had done when I was younger.

Everyone always "can" or "may" use the restroom.

They don't even need to ask.

My English as a second language students, all immigrants, like to hear stories of my name.

During my teenage years, I wished I had a simple American name, but I have learned to truly love my name.

The love I hold for my name now is evident as I tell them to be proud of their culture, families, and their names.

The classroom discussions about our heritage always end with them asking me to write my entire name on the board.

It goes like this: Cuba Vivian Fabiola de Fatima Pérez Silva Amargos Herrera Bonachea Castro Herrada Herrera Palmero Céspedes Prieto Núñez Rivadeneira.

What a mouthful!

Through my teaching, I stress the importance of assimilating into their new American culture, while always keeping their native culture dear to their hearts.

It is a new age.

Our world is filled with computers, the internet, social media, and cell phones.

I like to explore the possibilities they bring.

I am just learning how to navigate these new, unknown avenues of knowledge.

I have tried to use them, unsuccessfully, to find Lu or information about her.

I have not heard from her in years, but I have not forgotten her.

My hope that I will be able to find her again grows as I see the computer age take off.

With help from my family's younger generation, I have looked
   extensively for her.
Still, nothing comes up.
All I have is her name.
The powerful Iron Curtain remains strong.

However, my hope remains alive.

MAMY & CUBY

MRS. GIBLIN'S CLASS

SILVA FAMILY REUNIONS

Chapter 98

Hidden High Heels

It started with the shaking of his hands

His mouth unable to produce the words he so desperately wanted to say.

The loss of balance and the falling almost daily.

Parkinson's was killing my father.

It took all of him until he was left bedridden and on a feeding tube.

Mamy cared for him, bathed him, fed him, cleaned him, changed him, and loved him to no end. Not once did she ever waver in her steadfast devotion to him.

She was barely five feet tall and 100 pounds, yet she had the strength and dedication to continue to take him for years from his bed to the living room daily.

Then back to their room at night.

Until one day during my usual visit after work, something felt wrong.

I noticed Papy in his La-Z-Boy.

His color was off.

I knew he was gone, but through tears I performed CPR on his weak body.

Mamy was in the kitchen.

She didn't know.

I told her to call the ambulance.

It was too late.

Papy was gone.

The world had lost a true gentleman, a true scholar, and an amazing father.

No other person on this Earth has loved me as much as him.

Mamy died of Alzheimer's.

I am reminded of her daily.

Talking about this terrible disease still shakes me to my core.

It showed no mercy — it persisted, and despite all of our efforts, it won.

In the beginning, sometimes others would laugh at her when she would make mistakes or forget.

It pained me to watch.

After Papy died, I don't think a day went by that I didn't see my mother.

She moved in with me, then Cormac and his wife Lisa built a guesthouse at their home for her.

She loved living with her great-grandchildren Keagan and Kenzie next door.

Her great-grandchildren would run into her house every chance they had.

Mamy was caught several times trying to teach them to love chocolate and cows.

Later, Mamy went to live with Monet and Tommy in their guesthouse.

Her greatest joy was being with her family.

Her grandchildren and great-grandchildren brought such happiness to her.

She was always up for anything.

I don't know how she had so much energy.

Every summer I would book a vacation with Mamy.

We visited Europe, Alaska, the Caribbean.

We traveled the world together.

We visited so many beautiful places, but they became more and more difficult.

I, in a strange way, became her mother.

I was now her caregiver.

I would take her hand, feed her, and make sure she had everything she needed.

She could go nowhere without me.

If I left her side for a second, she would panic and not know what to do.

As her disease progressed, we would find her writing the names of places and people on her photographs.

Journaling in spiral notebooks — she wrote down everything she did, even though she spent most of her days alone waiting for anyone to visit.

No matter how long my daily visits would last, usually a few hours, she was always sad for me to go.

She would say, "But you're leaving already? You haven't even been here for long."

That was the only time she would complain.

She had a ritual of jumping up and down while waving as she watched my car pull away.

The pain of leaving her alone was unbearable.

Mamy began cutting up photos and taping them to her walls.

She would plaster them on like wallpaper.

The house was covered with memories that she desperately tried to cling to.

Almost daily I would walk into her home and she would be in tears.
As soon as she noticed me, Mamy would quickly try to hide them.
Even with her mind failing her, she showed the grace and class of
a queen.

She would take short walks but forget where she was and how to
get back.
In the end, she could not even make it to her mailbox without
getting lost.
The firefighters from the station down the street would often bring
her home.
Neny tried for sixteen years to find the right combination for her
medicine.
Sadness, depression, confusion, and frustration consumed her.
At times she would laugh, and I would see glimpses of my mother.
But in the end, it was her eyes that told the story.
She was helplessly trapped inside her own mind.
Martica was hired to help her with her daily life as she became
more and more mentally incapacitated.
In her later years, Mamy would still apply her red lipstick daily, do
her hair, put on her *tacones,* and wait for us to visit.
We always tried to hide her high heels when we left.
Tacones are too dangerous when you are 88.

When we would take her out, she always carried her empty
pocketbook.
She also brought a set of keys that only unlocked doors from
long ago.

I was tired and scared.
She could not live by herself.

Basic hygiene was forgotten.

Her body enabled her to do anything, but her mind was that of a child.

The dangers she presented to herself were constant.

The smell of burnt toast was always present in Monet's guesthouse, and her medication had to be hidden.

She needed twenty-four-hour care.

We felt the nursing home was the only option.

That proved to be the hardest and worst decision of my life.

Mamy died at the age of 91.

The world lost a truly selfless woman, a true hero, a true angel.

Mamy & Papy

I DID NOT HAVE TIME TO SAY GOODBYE

I DID NOT HAVE TIME TO SEE THE CUBAN SUN
ONCE AGAIN SHINING IN THE EARLY MORNINGS.
I DID NOT HAVE TIME TO SEE OUR MOON
LIGHTING THE BEAUTIFUL NIGHTS OF OUR COUNTRY
ONE LAST TIME.
I DID NOT HAVE TIME TO SAY GOODBYE TO
THE PALM TREES OF OUR CUBAN FIELDS
WHO SOLIDLY STAND ERECT AWAITING OUR RETURN.
I DID NOT HAVE TIME TO SAY GOODBYE.
—CUBA PÉREZ-AMARGOS

Chapter 99

America the Beautiful

I am proud to be an American.

I feel extreme love, pride, and allegiance to this nation — the greatest of all.

I have witnessed and cherished its triumphs.

I have also witnessed its times of despair and misery.

My family is living the American dream.

I stress to my students the beauty of the melting pot, where regardless of race, color, or creed, all are accepted.

Women are gaining ground.

Americans persevered and united nearly two hundred years before me to form our United States of America.

I cry joyful tears when American athletes sweep Olympic events.

I jump for joy when I learn that yet another Nobel Prize has been won by an American.

I marvel at the amazing inventors and inventions that leave me in awe.

I get shivers watching newly elected Presidents take their oath of office in our capitol.

I am inspired by the grandeur, majesty, and glory of our country's breathtaking natural sights.

I have also felt the painful moments.

My heart ached as I witnessed, with a classroom full of students, Christa McAuliffe, the brave teacher who was chosen to go into space, and the rest of the crew aboard the *Challenger* perish.

The terror of the twin towers falling on 9-11 is an open wound I carry that will never be healed.

Race riots and racial inequalities leave me with questions without answers.

Yet, I am free to be me, and I thank you, America the Beautiful — the United States of America.

ALEX

CHUCHIN

RYAN

JORGE

SCOTT

ENRIQUE

Chapter 100

Family

Brian and I divorced.

I was alone.

I entered a tunnel with no visible exit.

Then, one day, after a long, long time of distress and sorrow, I received a book from my daughter Sterling.

Inside was the quote, "Dance like no one is watching. Sing like no one is listening. Love like you've never been hurt. And live like it's heaven on Earth."

I cried.

I was free again.

I have forgiven.

I have earned my master's in education.

I remember my father's words about education and pass them along to my children.

They all graduated from the University of Florida and Florida State University with their master's degrees and doctorates.

They received degrees in political science, education, and veterinary medicine.

Papy would be so proud.

I went to my Notre Dame High School reunion with Monet, Sterling, and Brian.

I loved catching up with all our Connecticut friends.

We saw all the loving Giblins, too.

It is amazing to go back in time with the knowledge I possess now.

I see much of myself in my children.

Cormac has the confidence and self-assurance that I possessed as a child.

He knows what he wants and how to get it.

He is an eloquent speaker — I watch him speak on television discussing our county's issues.

Monet has a creativity and skill for teaching and photography.

We have taught together in Immokalee, a migrant community in Collier County, Florida.

She loves the beach, swimming, and competing at anything from races to board games.

Sterling shares my passion for animals.

She has become a veterinarian and helps animals of all kinds, even the strays.

Her hospital's doors remain open to all — regardless of circumstances.

From an early age she has possessed a unique gift that calms and heals animals.

Her favorite pet was Pinky the Pig, who won first prize at the pet contest when she was seven.

"Pinky don't come, Pinky don't sit …."

The judges loved the two of them.

She came home with a trophy bigger than her.

I am blessed I did not have to say goodbye to my children.

We all live in Naples, Florida.

Our family has expanded to include the Fugates, the Laytons, the Sigmonds, and the Williamsons.

Jake, Brady, and Laney are always part of all the festivities, now that Cormac and Lisa have divorced and he and Ashley are together.

We enjoy every holiday from Martin Luther King, Jr., Day, where we watch the parade and party in the park, to New Year's Day where we meet at the beach for grapes and champagne as we each send our wishes to the world.

We even celebrate el Día de los Inocentes on December 28. I always am able to trick my grandchildren on this Cuban version of April Fool's Day, because they never remember when it is.

Hurricanes bring us all together, too.

Sometimes sixteen of us and our animals hunker down to ride out the storm.

Although the wind howls and the rain pounds, we are not afraid.

Scott is our five-star chef, Vanden the entertainment, Tommy checks for any leaks, and Cormac checks on the status of the storm.

Havana, the weather reporter, makes live video updates to send to relatives who are anxious to hear about the storm.

Catalina and Eire are sure to come up with new activities and games for us to play, while Monet and Sterling brainstorm creative ideas.

We swim in the pool and dance outside as the eye of Irma passes.

Electricity and air conditioning are not needed to have fun.

After the storm passes the kids rush out to make forts with the large fallen branches.

I help keep the house in order and enjoy the time together.

My daughters throw the best parties around for their children.

They would rival any Silva shindig in Havana.

Six beautiful grandchildren grace my life, five girls and one boy.
I treasure the moments I have with them.

Cormac and Lisa have Keagan and Kenzie.
Keagan is kind and compelled to see the world.
She chooses her own path, and she surprises me with her courage
     and independence.
Kenzie is full of laughter and always up for anything.
She is known for her dance moves.
She has a perpetual smile on her face, and she will do anything for
     anyone at any time all while enjoying the moment.

Sterling and Scott have Catalina and Vanden.
Catalina is smart, focused, and super creative.
She always has a book in her hand.
She is meticulous and sweet, and she has a quiet confidence.
Vanden is a wrecking ball.
He is a wild boy with a curious mind and a genuine heart.
He will do great things — that is certain.

Havana and Eire are Monet and Tommy's.
Havana has the flavor of Cuba in her spirit and in her name.
She continues the Silva tradition with a twist.
She inspires all around her by achieving greatness in all she does
     — she truly shines.
Eire is sporty, spunky, and stunningly beautiful.
She tells it like it is and wears her heart on her sleeve.

Eire dances like Lu, maybe even better.

Conga & Lu

Chapter 101

Grandchildren

The time I spend with my grandchildren is what I cherish the most in my life.

They call me Abita.

No matter what we are doing together, there's always laughs along the way.

We have sleepovers at my house many times throughout the year; most of them are for holidays.

We always try to schedule them for when Keagan is home from college.

Hours are spent together making drip sandcastles at the beach.

Vanden redesigns the living room and makes forts with my couch pillows.

I teach them canasta, and it takes me back to when I used to play as a child.

Havana waits for a hidden canasta, while Eire always blurts out when she has a mono or wild card in her hand.

The lake out back is always entertaining.

Eire, Catalina, and Vanden come back into the house with dirt covering their toes and clothes with frogs in their hands.

The poor creatures jump around, trying to escape from whatever experiments the mad scientists have planned.

The tadpoles they collect swim around in tiny glass jars.

Conga & Lu

We walk to Mel's Diner with our flashlights.
Eire refuses to go on the days that the ventriloquist is performing.
We play card games, dominoes, and Rummikub on the big glass
   table.
The children have art contests and spend hours doodling in their
   notebooks.
You can always count on Havana, Kenzie, and Keagan to make
   the cookies.
Sometimes we work on puzzles.
It is always frustrating when we can't find the last piece.
Usually it's found in the mouth of one of the dogs, Chunky and
   Julio Caliente, who are often caught nibbling on the one piece
   that we need.

The children have races with the dogs in the yard.
Julio Caliente Papi Chulo is always the fastest.
We have art contests and perform magic tricks.
We are still perfecting the art of making *croquetas*.
Everyone gathers around the glass table and prepares for the messy
   and tiring process.
Flour flies everywhere.
Vanden loses interest quickly, but it's worth the effort when we
   taste them.
Even Abuela would give her approval.

Every so often we visit the chapel at St. Ann Church and say our
   silent prayers.
Sometimes we meet at the mall to buy gifts for whomever has the
   next birthday.
We also have white elephant gift exchanges.

When it's time to go to bed, everyone always fights over the twin beds.

Keagan and Kenzie usually call dibs because they are the oldest.

Havana is always the first to wake up.

We all walk the dogs and then make breakfast.

French toast sticks, eggs, bacon, pancakes, Cuban bread, and orange juice.

If it's hot, we go straight to the pool.

We sing "London Bridge" when we shower after the pool.

Those who are already teens sing the loudest.

Sometimes Sterling and Monet join us for breakfast before they leave with the kids.

Every back to school, Valentine's Day, Halloween, and just about every holiday I make baskets for each of my grandkids.

They are loaded with candy, stuffed animals, and games.

I also never forget to send a card with a two-dollar bill for every holiday.

We keep the tradition of Cuban *Noche Buena* alive every year, just as we did in Cuba.

Thanks to Olga and Tony, the tradition made it to Naples.

We joined them at their house in Golden Gate Estates for years.

Now the Sigmonds are proud to host.

We gather family and friends and enjoy roast pork, yuca with plenty of mojo, black beans and rice, and sweet plantains.

There is so much food that everyone leaves with enough leftovers to last a week.

Tom and Peggy, Monet's in-laws, join us, too, and make sure no food is ever wasted!

Sometimes we have more than fifty people together celebrating.

We blend old traditions with new ones.

My favorite new tradition is the song and dance my grandchildren perform.

Keagan is usually the choreographer, and Vanden the director and emcee.

It is a highlight of the night when they perform on Christmas Eve.

My favorite act ever was when they sang "Guantanamera," each reciting a verse of José Martí's poems from "*Versos Sencillos.*"

Jake, Brady, and Laney even got in on the act.

Christmas is one of the happiest days of the year.

Presents of all shapes and sizes fill the living room.

All of the children find their bags loaded with gifts.

Everyone comes from Brian's house, and it's always a race to my house.

It's always close between the Giblins and the Sigmonds, but the Laytons (or the "Late Ones") usually come in last.

Eire and Havana always complain that Tommy drives too slowly.

Tommy reminds them they are "fashionably Layton," adding, "Better Layton than never."

Julio and Chunky look through the window, barking and wagging their tails as people run to the door.

"The children are here!" I say.

We eat brunch; then the gift opening begins.

Bags labeled for everyone are filled with thoughtful tokens of love.

Laughter fills the house, and scattered shreds of torn gift wrap cover the tile floor.

Tommy is always the first to initiate the cleanup.

The best gift I have ever received is the ability to spend so much time with my grandchildren.

They keep my heart beating.

Chapter 102

On in Years

I live on D'Strampes Street, just two blocks
from Figueroa. Many of the apartments and
homes are not in good shape. Supplies are very
hard to find. There are no tools or paint. Our
apartment building is many different colors.
People use whatever paint they can find at the
time. Each tenant paints their own. I have not
been able to paint mine in years. I still get
up every morning, turn the radio on, and move
as I sweep and clean our apartment. Our place
may not have the most modern conveniences,
but I polish it and make it sparkle daily. The
ceiling fans help us survive the Cuban heat.

Our small apartment has seen tears, shared
in our happiness, and been good to us. I am
so proud of the men and women my children
have become.

They have all finished school and graduated.
They are all professionals. Barbara is a blood
technician. She works to help our health
systems through the blood bank. Elena, also in
the health field, is sometimes called abroad
as nations such as Angola need medical support
from the Cuban government. I live here with

Barbara. She has unfortunately been cursed with the same bad luck with men that I have had my whole life. Barbara is a single mom but has given me grandchildren. I am overjoyed that I am now also now a great-grandmother.

Nathaly, my great-granddaughter, is the light of my life. When Nathaly visits, I come alive. She keeps me smiling. On the weekends I go to my daughter Elena's house. She lives on the other side of the neighborhood. We all get together on Sundays.

My advanced age has not suppressed my tasty cooking skills. I enjoy cooking. I prepare a family dinner with whatever food we have — usually rice, beans, and plantains. I usually mix *fideos* into the rice, so that we have more food to pass around. I also still very much enjoy eating. Coffee is not widely available, but we sit and enjoy a cup together after dinner. I can no longer sew. My eyes grow tired, and the arthritis in my hands is painful at times.

I still pass the time watching people go by from my balcony. I reminisce about the old days when I first came to Havana. Barbara has tried to help me locate Conga. She is able to access a computer at her job. She has had no luck. She found a René Pérez on Facebook, and I thought it might be Neny, but it was not.

I think of my Conga often. I miss her letters. She would send me cards for Mother's

Day, birthdays, and New Year's. She sent me her wedding announcement and even sent us stockings for Christmas one year. Her Papy, Señor René, sent a letter, too. He had asked me to come to America. I wrote back to him and told him I could never leave my family or country. I have not received a letter from my Conga in many years. But she remains close to my heart. She must have children and maybe even grandchildren by now. I never forget her.

ELENA   NATHALY   WILLIAM   ELENA

BARBARA & NATHALY   LU

Chapter 103

Going Home

It is November 9, 2018, and I am going home.
After fifty-seven long years.
Travel to Cuba has opened.
Flights are running between Ft. Lauderdale and Havana.

I have waited months to receive the papers from the Cuban government
that will allow me to travel back since I left as an exile in 1961.
It is easier for my daughters, Monet and Sterling, to travel.
My bags are packed.
I can't sleep.
I cannot believe it.

I have all the places I want to visit in my mind.
I don't need a map.
I can remember it like yesterday.
My whole neighborhood.
The drive to Vedado.
Miramar Yacht Club.
The *finca*.
I am ready.

We drive from Naples to Fort Lauderdale.
We board the Jet Blue plane that will fly us to Havana in less than
an hour.
Finally, I WILL BE HOME.

We land in Havana and have to wait for hours for our bags.

The airport is hot and loud.

Cubans are waiting for the purchases they made in Miami.

It looks like a layaway in Walmart.

There are TVs, weedwhackers, toasters, bedding, all wrapped tightly in blue plastic.

Cubans are expert packers.

They fit an unbelievable amount of goods into one package.

The wait for our bags doubles that of our flight

We are worried we may be stuck here all night.

People are pushing and shoving.

We wait and wait, then finally we exchange our dollars for CUCs and are ready to go.

The air is just as I remember.

It is fresh, not humid or hot.

The sun shines on my face.

The palm leaves sway in the wind as if they are waving hello to me.

Cuba has been stuck in time.

It is a paradise that has been left behind.

A place that time forgot.

There is a special feeling, a mystical wonder in the air.

We get a driver and cruise around with the top down.

I see the beauty in the Havana sky.

We see the massive walls that helped protect Havana from its invaders over the centuries.

Children are walking home from school, all in uniform.

Red pants or skirts and white shirts.

We pass two soldiers on the corner, guns in hand.

We see waves crashing over the *Malecón*.
The *Hotel Nacional* is kept very well.
The antique American cars are the same as when I had left.
I see the building where my parents and Abuelo worked.
We enter *el bosque*, "the lungs of Havana."
It is like a mini rainforest — green ivy and vines cover all the trees.
The air is so pure that it cleanses us.
I remember the last birthday party I had in Cuba was here.
It is a magical place.

We drive through Chinatown, where I used to get the best ice
    cream.
It's as if time stopped when I left.
We decide to stop and get some ice cream.
There is one side that has many flavors for tourists.
The other side is for locals, and they only have three flavors to
    choose from.

Old Havana has been preserved.
I never really went there, though.
I remember taking a field trip to the *Plaza de la Catedral* in
    first grade.
It was creepy for me to be in buildings that were built in the 1500s.
They were too old, too dark, and smelled of urine.
As we walk the wooden streets, I still smell urine.
We see many tourists and tour guides here.
Peddlers selling flowers, *empanadas*, and rum approach us.
They are looking for American dollars.
The black market, or *bolsa negra*, has become a big part of the
    Cuban economy.
Bands play and sing José Martí's famous words:

Guantanamera, guajira, Guantanamera
Guantanamera, guajira, Guantanamera.

Old Havana is colorful, vibrant, beautiful.
But within blocks there is much decay, devastation, and desperation.
Stray dogs roam with signs around their necks that say, "Please
    don't kick me."
Buildings struggle to remain upright.
We hand out candy to some children.
Their smiles are brighter than the sun.

We will stay in El Vedado tonight at a bed-and-breakfast home.
The sidewalks are the same ones that I had played hopscotch on
    after school over fifty years ago.
But my school is gone.
The walls are gone, and it is a shell of a building.
Heaps of rubble fill what used to be the courtyard.
The remaining windows are either shattered or adorned with
    iron bars.

We go to the *Tropicana* nightclub.
We sit in the open-air balcony and watch the scantily clad women
    dance to the songs the live band plays.
They bring us rum and chocolates.
I picture my parents coming here in the 1950s with their friends,
    laughing, enjoying themselves before everything changed.
Tomorrow we will stay in a *casa particular* in La Víbora.

I am finally here, but strangely I still feel so far away.

Conga & Lu

HAVANA

Chapter 104

Lost in My Own Home

My once-beautiful neighborhood looks like a war zone.
Schools are deteriorating, missing whole walls, and roofs are gone.
Paint is peeling.
Yards are filled with weeds.
People are still outside, sitting, talking, and smiling.
We stop to talk to some strangers who are gardening.
I thought they would be unkind to me once they found out that
    I had left in the 1960s.
They are not.
They are kind, welcoming, and interested in my story.

I turn the corner.
I recognize the pillars at once.
CARDECUYOTU.
My home.
It is struggling to stand.
The pillars are crumbling.
It is painted orange, white, and purple, and there are bits of
    turquoise peeking through.
Oh, how I miss its majestic white frame.
The porch where Abuelo Delio once sat and rocked is home to a
    broken car with no wheels.
My heart aches.
My eyes fill with tears.

The tiny apartment on top of the garage where Lu lived is barely
recognizable.
We wave at an elderly woman who is outside on what used to be
Carmenchu's porch upstairs.
I tell her I lived here fifty-seven years ago.
She smiles and invites us in.
We go upstairs to the left and through the hall.
"Come inside," she says.
No Silvas are left at CARDECUYOTU, but we meet Elda.
She remembers my Abuelo Delio, my grandfather, who had stayed
here in our house until he died.
The government let Elda and her family move into the house
in 1962.

I see my grandmother's French bedroom set in Elda's apartment.
She says a woman named Angela, who moved in after we fled, had
given it to her.
She explains how many families have come and gone through the
years.
She has been there the longest.
We talk about the different people who have inhabited my house.
She has been here throughout the decades.
She heard stories about me and all the Silvas from my abuelo.

She gives us Cuban coffee, ham, and cheese.
She even breaks out a bottle of wine.
We eat on aluminum foil airline trays.
I sit in a lawn chair instead of the gorgeous upholstered dining
chairs that once sat at the beautiful mahogany table.
We sit and talk as my head spins in this surreal moment.
I am here in CARDECUYOTU.

It doesn't feel like home.
I am crushed.

She tells me my abuelo was such a wonderful man.
She pulls out a photo of him.
I know she has much admiration and respect for him.

She shows us around the rest of the house.
So much has changed.
Sterling videotapes as Monet snaps photos.
I try to fight back tears.
They have separated CARDECUYOTU into eight different houses.
There are eight different families living here.

Very little of what I know remains.
I enter my house and am greeted by Lourdes.
She tells me her family moved into the house in 1970, when she
    was just six years old.
The roof in my bedroom is falling in.
The bedroom which my mother had painstakingly decorated is
    barely recognizable.
The corner where I kept my play kitchen is now home to a hot plate.
My room is now the kitchen of its new tenant, Lourdes.
She apologizes for the condition of the home.
She explains that materials are almost impossible to find, and she
    cannot fix all that needs repaired.

Nothing is the same.
My dolls, clothes, record player — all gone.
The wall of shelves that had once been home to all our toys from
    Spain and France is riddled with mold and cracks.

The window valances our seamstress had custom designed that
once read "Cuby and Reny" disappeared long ago.
Water drips from above into a bucket.

Mamy and Papy's beautiful oriental-style bedroom has vanished.
Their master bedroom and our old kitchen is now another
apartment.
Materials and paint are very expensive and tough to find.
Much is left to the elements.
The house is crumbling.
A small dog barks at us; he is tied to where our fireplace had
been.

My home, which once was as grand as a castle, is unidentifiable.
I don't want to see any more.
Each door that opens reveals one heartbreak after another.
There are walls separating our spacious home, creating new rooms
everywhere.
I am lost in my own house.

All the gracious tenants come outside to meet us.
We meet Darlen, who is Lourdes' niece.
She lives in the back of our old house.
Darlen gives us a papier-mâché parrot that she has made.
What's theirs is ours — they are the kindest souls.
They are all so very thoughtful and eager to learn about my
experiences.
They welcome us with open arms.
Elda explains I was the girl who was forced to flee.
We leave them with some candy and chocolates.

We see the apartments that have been created downstairs.
Our lower level has been transformed into four more apartments.
The grand entrance and never-ending hallway are missing, too.
Inside we find a motorcycle and its parts on the black-and-white
marble floor.
I smile because it is the same floor — I can recognize it.
A young girl and her family live in the room that used to be
Chuchin's.
She is about six.
We give her a doll and some candy.

I can't bear anymore.
Glimpses of my childhood play peek-a-boo with me through the
cracks in the drywall.
I try to envision my dreamy first ten years of life here.
I cannot believe what it has become.
Outside in the back yard the mamey tree is gone.
Clothes hang drying in the sun.
Lu's apartment is dilapidated and unlivable.
The iron staircase is completely missing.
I can't even believe this is the same home I had left so long ago.
Sadness consumes me and it is hard to speak.
It is time to go.

I am afraid to ask, but I must.
"Elda, do you know what happened to Iluminada? She was my
manejadora when I lived here. We had exchanged letters for
years, but it has been decades since I have heard from her."
"Ah, yes, I remember Iluminada. I have not seen her in quite some
time," she says. "The last I heard she was living in an apartment

building not too far from here. But it has been many years
since I have seen her."
She scribbles an address on an old piece of mail.
"This is where I last know she lived."
"Gracias, adios," I tell her.

I whisper, "Goodbye, CARDECUYOTU."
As I depart, I leave a kiss on a pillar.

The address is just around the corner.
My heart sinks and soars at the same time.
Has it been too long?
Will my Lu still be here?
She would now be eighty-four years old, if she is still alive.
I am sixty-seven and last saw her smiling eyes when I was ten.
I fear the worst racing up the uneven streets that I used to walk
as a child.

My emotions overcome me.

CARDECUYOTU

Chapter 105

A Hundred Goodbyes

I turn the corner.
We are just houses away from the address on the paper.
I don't even notice that I am walking.
Monet points up ahead.
"Is that her?" Sterling asks.
There are three women standing on a second-floor balcony.
"Iluminada Vidal?" I shout
"Yes," the oldest one answers.
"It's me, Conga!" My voice shaking.
"Conga?" she says, her voice is strong.
Her reply sends me into a dreamlike state.

We rush ahead.
As we get closer, I see the tears form in her eyes.
I see her smile, still shining like a light, the gold at the end of a rainbow.
Her hair is up in a colorful kerchief.

My Lu.
This time SHE is upstairs by her banister.
She lives on the second floor.
We get closer and sprint upstairs.
The door is already open.
My heart leaps from my body.
My Lu.

We stare at each other and embrace.

I am wrapped in her loving arms once again.

Her face has changed, but her eyes still twinkle.

Her deep dimples remain.

My young, vibrant Lu is now a great-grandmother.

She is 84 years old.

Her voice is calming and sweet.

It takes me back.

I am a child, and we are dancing together, laughing, playing Parcheesi on the floor.

"But, how are you here? You found me!" she says.

We tell her how we had just visited CARDECUYOTU, and Elda had given us her address.

She tells me tales of what I was like when I was young.

I relive my whole childhood in three hours.

She reveals to my daughters that I was the smallest but the spunkiest of all the children in the house.

"I think I only had to scold you one time," she says. "I put you in *penitencia* (time out) for fighting with your brother. You were a pistol that day. You really hurt him! When your father got home, he said 'I'm sure she deserved it.'"

She confesses that she would cheat when I played canasta with her.

No wonder she always won.

She asks about Neny.

I tell her Mamy and Papy are gone.

I cannot believe that her two daughters are here and mine are here, too.

Our reunion is beyond wonderful.

415

She shares stories about my *abuelo*.
He was the only Silva who had remained in CARDECUYOTU.
Lu and her family were with him until the day he died.
Lu's daughter Barbara recounts many stories of the time she cherished with him.
They all remember him so fondly.

We share stories, pictures, laughs, and tears.
She points to her leg and shows us the scar she got when she tried to ride Tormenta.
We laugh and laugh.
She tells me pieces of my youth that I had forgotten.
She brings out a large weathered envelope.
She opens it to reveal all the letters and the few photos I have sent her throughout the years.
She has kept them all.

She shows me my wedding announcement from the newspaper that I had mailed her.
Once we both moved and addresses were changed, the letters stopped.
While we talk, I realize she did not have my correct address once we moved to Florida, and I had no idea she was not living in CARDECUYOTU any longer.
It has been over forty years since we have heard from each other.

I get to know her daughters, Barbara and Elena.
As Barbara recounted the wonderful life she had shared with Abuelo Delio as a child, the pain and sadness I had carried all these years lifted.

416

Abuelo Delio had more than a dozen years of joyful bliss with Barbara and Elena, the little girls he had come to love.

The years I had envisioned Abuelo feeling lonely and alone were wiped away by the memories these beautiful women shared with us and who had come into his life the moment he needed it most.

I love that Monet and Sterling can meet Lu and her family.
Lu also tells me about grandchildren and great-granddaughter, Nathaly.
I show her pictures of my grandchildren on my cell phone.

We talk of happiness, love, and hardships.
We are so happy, we weep.
I am finally reunited with my Lu, and she is reunited with her Conga.
We chat, chuckle, and cry together.
Hours seem like minutes.

Once again, I must leave.
But this time I get to say farewell.
I'm not sure which instance is harder.
We say a hundred goodbyes and give a thousand kisses.
I don't know if it will be the last time I see her.
We live such a short distance on a map, but our countries are worlds away from each other.

I leave gifts for her and her family — toiletries, candy, and clothes.
We had selected some items from the Dollar Store in Florida to give to the children of the island.
I picked some favorites from my childhood — gum, Silly Putty, coloring books.
We have passed them out during our visit.

Our bag of goodies is almost gone.
I reach inside and pull out the last item, a tiny bag.
Inside, a shiny set of new jacks.
It's as if God himself had left them in there.
"For Nathaly," I say.

The jacks bring me back to the first day I met Iluminada Vidal.
My Lu.

Conga and Lu.

STERLING, MONET, ELENA
LU, CONGA, BARBARA

LU

ELENA, LU, CONGA,& BARBARA

CONGA & LU

Epilogue

It had been fifty-seven years since I had left Cuba, my homeland. But the Cuba I had left as a child had been with me my entire life. My Cuba is the smell of garlic and olive oil simmering in the frying pan. It is the taste of each *cafecito* I drink. It is every hand of canasta I now play with my grandchildren. It is the language that rolls off my tongue when all my family gets together. It is the sound of frogs croaking at dusk. It is the fronds of the royal palms swaying in the breeze.

I never left my Cuba. My Cuba cannot be changed, destroyed, or broken.

I carry it with me daily.

It is now within the pages of this book.

I am Cuba.

Dedication

This is dedicated to the Silvas, who with hearts full of hope and love left their beloved island. They carried the love of family instilled in them by Abuelo Delio and Abuela Cuba. Thank you for the sufferings and hardships you endured. We are forever indebted to you. You made us who we are today.

Acknowledgments

The stories and memories captured in this book are an honest and true account of what happened in the lives of the characters.

Thank you to all our family and friends who helped create the wonderful memories that are the heart of this book — your stories and lives have changed ours forever. We love you all.

This book would not be possible without the support and love from Iluminada Vidal and her daughter, Barbara Megret. After meeting in Havana, reminiscing, and sharing tales from years not forgotten, we were able to keep in contact. Through phone calls, letters, and social media, Iluminada provided the details, anecdotes, and information that were used to write the chapters about her life. It is her voice that is heard.

To Tom and Peggy Layton, thank you for your insights and suggestions along the way.

Thank you to Tommy for your help in editing and constant love and support.

A special thank you to Havana for all the editing and for writing Chapter 101, the beautiful chapter about grandchildren.

Thank you to Cormac for filling in the gaps and for the missing pieces.

Also, thank you to Brian, Sterling, Eire, Keagan, Kenzie, Catalina, and Vanden, who were always eager to hear the next chapters.

Thank you to El Pillo and Aleida, Carmencita Silva, and Susana Toledo for opening our eyes to what has and is happening in Cuba now.

Conga & Lu

Thank you to Carmen, Jorge, Natalie, Renecito, Elena, and Lourdes for providing us with some of the priceless photos that were included in this book. Getting photos from Iluminada of her family in Cuba during the '70s and '80s was real challenge. There was not much opportunity to buy or develop film for her. We are thankful to have the treasures she was able to share.

Authors' Note

"Everyone is happy now, but later all will cry."
— Dr. Delio Silva Castro, 1959

And the crying continues for the Cuban people after more than sixty years of oppression by the Cuban government. Their liberties and most basic human rights are being undeniably stripped. Violence and torture are used to control and persecute, and their freedom is taken. The Cuban people sadly do not have the freedom to honestly express their gut-wrenching views. Their eyes and averted glances, however, tell the brutal story — the story that their words cannot.

About the Authors

Born Cuba Perez-Silva, author Cuba Giblin left Havana in 1961 at the age of ten, one of over 14,000 unaccompanied minors that fled Cuba's Communist regime through Operacíon Pedro Pan. She has since been devoted to the memories of her family's Cuban roots and culture. After living in Miami, Florida, and Bridgeport, Connecticut, Cuba attended the University of Connecticut and the University of Bridgeport, where she received her Bachelor of Arts degree. She later gradu-

ated from Florida Gulf Coast University with a Master's in Elementary Education, specializing in Reading for a Diverse Society. For the last forty years, Cuba has enjoyed teaching kindergarten through twelfth grade, as well as adult education. She is a National Board-Certified teacher. Happily retired in Naples, Florida, she enjoys nature walks, reading, and living in the present moment. She is surrounded and uplifted by her children and grandchildren, who continue to keep her stories and traditions alive.

Author Monet Layton was born in Connecticut and grew up in Florida. After receiving her Master's in Elementary Education from the University of Florida, she worked as a kindergarten and first-grade teacher. She is now a photographer and co-owns Naples Coastal Art with her "cousin," Emma Casagrande. Monet is also a high school swim coach. She's married to Tommy, who she knows is a far better author than her. They live in Naples, Florida, with their two incredible daughters, Havana and Eire, and their TV-watching wonder dog Kessel. She loves the beach, Cuban food (especially *ropa vieja*), photography, party games, teaching, her daily phone calls with Sterling, traditions, Thursday coffees, being in the water, and above all else, her family.

Monet Layton

Havana Layton

CPSIA information can be obtained
at www.ICGtesting.com
Printed in the USA
LVHW090904240723
753027LV00079B/27